MICHAEL FLANDERS

AT THE DOFF[1] OF A HAT

An affectionate tribute

Richard R. Dolphin

1st impression: March 2023

2nd impression: June 2023

---

[1] To remove your hat as a sign of respect

Richard. R. Dolphin

Photograph Hilary Johne Lake

Richard R. Dolphin

is an author and lecturer

*

His enthusiasms include steam locomotives and drinking real ale in proper English pubs.

*

When not restoring his ancient country house, he can be found reading political biography, chopping down trees, pointing walls, taking his much-loved Old English sheepdog for walks; and, in season, plucking pheasants.

for Christine

A. [signature]

21/vii/23

INTRODUCTION

In late December 1957 my Uncle Bert and Auntie Marjorie invited me to stay with them for a week in outer London. As the son of an impoverished minister of religion, I was taken to places and events that I had never imagined. The highlight was being taken to the Fortune Theatre in Covent Garden to see *At the Drop of a Hat*.[2] I can picture it still: and remember my aunt and uncle's horror at the lyrics 'Bloody January again'. It was wonderful. I followed Flanders and Swann throughout the rest of their lives.

Claudia Flanders was working on a biography of her husband when she died. Swann wrote an account of *his* life. This short text is intended to be an appreciation - if you like - of Flanders and to give a little information about where he went and what he did; until a more substantive text becomes available.

So, this text is not intended to be more than a reminder of the main events of Flanders' life: in that respect I hope

---

[2] If you do something at the drop of a hat, you do it immediately without stopping to think about it

that it might engender enthusiasm and interest from those who remember him as one of the great theatrical heroes of the last century: one of those people that one simply admired.

During his career he made innumerable broadcasts of all kinds on radio and television; at one stage he was chairman of *The Brains Trust*. He wrote the libretti of two operas; translated (with Kitty Black) Stravinsky's *The Soldier's Tale* - and in 1962 appeared as The Storyteller in the Royal Shakespeare Company's production of Brecht's *The Caucasian Chalk Circle* at the Aldwych. In 1964 he received the OBE.

His daughter said that her memory of him was shaped by his public persona. In private, she said, he was very different. "He was not an ogre, but people were sometimes disappointed because he wasn't terribly witty all the time. They would come round to dinner and expect it to be like the show. But, of course, all the spontaneous things in the show had been carefully choreographed and rehearsed. He was a smart, acerbic[3] guy."[4]

Brian Sibley recalls that he went to a retrospective show at the National Film Theatre celebrating the work of

---

[3] To be sharp or biting
[4] https://www.telegraph.co.uk/culture/tvandradio/3587226/Ill-give-as-good-as-I-get.html

the musical comedy duo, Flanders and Swann.[5] Despite the fact that the archive footage was almost entirely in black and white and with all the fuzziness of 405-lines,[6] this was an evening of pure blissful delight.

This appreciation is not intended to be an attempt at a biography. No one who worked with Flanders – or his family – have been approached. At times the narrative may seem like a catalogue of events. What it is intended to do is to demonstrate through an examination of the work that Flanders performed - and the programmes in which he appeared - what an extraordinarily talented and brave man he was.

This writer does not believe that pundits associate Flanders with verse. Yet he appeared in many programmes focussed on poetry; particularly is his early days of broadcasting. Just as in his later years he appeared in a number of religious programmes; yet few people reflect on this aspect of his life.

Then, taking up that point, it is amazing how someone whose career was cut off at the knees through illness managed to carve out a replacement career in double quick time and turned it into an enormous international

---

[5] http://briansibleysblog.blogspot.com/2008/02/who-says-nostalgia-isnt-what-it-was.html
[6] The number of lines influences the quality of the picture

success. Part of this story of accomplishment is demonstrated by his regular appearances on all sorts of radio shows: many in the pre-television days (in the sense that televisions were not found in very many homes until the 1953 coronation).

Flanders would have been in his mid-twenties going on thirty in this era and the number of programmes for children and young people in which he appeared is noteworthy. Yet, there is no recorded evidence of his being particularly interested in this age group.

Classical music critic and broadcaster John Amis was famous for his summer schools for musicians: first at Bryanston School and later at Dartington: those schools seem largely forgotten. But if it had not been for Swann appearing at Dartington: and there being a wheelchair-bound person in the organizational office, Flanders himself might never have been invited down. Had he not attended he and Swann would never have been asked to entertain the patrons. Without that exposure they would not have enjoyed a readymade audience for their opening night at the New Lindsey Theatre. It is all the stuff of serendipity.

Then again, this writer believes that most admirers of Flanders would associate him in their mind with Swann:

but not with translating. Yet he was clearly a gifted linguist and, almost without anyone noticing, he put this talent to recognizable use.

Lastly, in terms of his wheelchair, there could be no better example of what this writer's mother used to call "turning a liability into an asset". We are told that Flanders was initially shy of appearing on stage with an obvious disability. Yet within a decade and a half he had turned the wheelchair into an identifiable and measurable tool of his trade; almost perhaps a prop.

His loss to British theatre reverberates down through the years: but we look back on his life with much gratitude: not just for the immeasurable pleasure that he brought to so many diverse people but also for the bravery and self-discipline that he practiced in everything that he did.

PREAMBLE

I have referred to both Flanders and Swann by their surnames throughout this text. That is the style that was prevalent when they were performing and it was, in any case, how they referred to each other.

Readers may assume that all radio and television appearances were broadcast by the BBC: unless the text indicates otherwise.

CHAPTER ONE

Michael Henry Flanders was a many-faceted polymath. He was genial and mild;[7] a big, burly man described by one old friend as looking "like a great, lovable beached whale not at all delicate and sickly" even though he had been confined to a wheelchair since 1943.[8] Flanders' first Wardrobe Mistress - that was a joke, she was the stage manager - Carole-Ann Aylett[9] commented of him that "he was very much the playboy: very charismatic and sexy". She went on, "He used to chase me around in his chair".[10] In his impossibly difficult circumstances he kept an unchallenged warmth and urbanity.[11]

Flanders appeared on stage, screen, radio, concert platforms and recordings. He wrote opera librettos, children's books, a volume of poetry and the words of a

---

[7] Amis, John: *Dropping the Hat Again*, Radio 2 documentary, 12th January 1997
[8] New York Times; obituary 1975
[9] Now 87: she had a successful career as an actress
[10] https://www.bbc.co.uk/sounds/play/b00d1025
[11] The Times: obituary 1975

cantata about Noah's Ark.¹² He was 'every inch a man of the theatre.'¹³ The writer might have added that, disability or not, he was every inch a real man's man. In fact, you might almost say that he demolished the word *disability* and gave it new meaning.

Flanders was born in Hampstead (where he lived with his mother for many years) on 1st March 1922 and was the only son of Peter Henry Flanders and his wife, Rose Laura Hastings. Dad was a theatre manager and Mum was a violinist and song writer.¹⁴ It was a winning combination.

From 1936-40 he was a charming¹⁵ pupil at Westminster School where he shone in athletics, rowing and (especially) school dramatics. Westminster was evacuated to Exeter University during the war and it was whilst there that Flanders devised, wrote, directed and acted in a school revue *Go to it!* – one of the great slogans of the War.¹⁶

Incidentally, one night during their London run twenty years later, the Headmaster from Westminster (who

---

¹² https://en.wikipedia.org/wiki/Michael_Flanders
¹³ Amis, John: Op. cit.
¹⁴ Swann, Donald: *Swann's Way*, Arthur James 1993, p. 134
¹⁵ https://www.filmedlivemusicals.com/drop-another-hat.html
¹⁶ Swann, Donald: Op. cit. p. 68

Flanders did not like) arrived at the stage door alongside Harold Macmillan. Flanders kept the HM waiting, as one does, while he talked to the Premier.[17]

While at Westminster, contemporaries included Anthony Wedgewood Benn (a lifelong friend: he was a stagehand in this play)[18] and Peter Ustinov.[19] Benn referred to Flanders then as a "very commanding figure: one with great presence."[20]

In 1940 Flanders went to Christ Church, Oxford to read History (where another mutual friend was Kenneth Tynan). There he both acted and directed for the dramatic society *and* the Experimental Theatre Club (ETC was founded in 1936 at Oxford University to explore new and challenging ways of creating theatre experiences).[21] Among many roles, he played Brabantio in *Othello*, Pirandello[22] in *Henry IV* and Shawcross in *The Ascent of F6*. He also wrote drama criticisms for the Oxford magazine *Cherwell*.[23]

---

[17] Amis, John: *Dropping the Hat Again*, Radio 2 documentary, 12th January 1997

[18] http://news.bbc.co.uk/1/hi/magazine/6253824.stm

[19] https://www.comedy.co.uk/features/comedy_chronicles/remarkable-legacy-of-flanders-and-swann/

[20] Amis, John: Op. cit.

[21] https://www.facebook.com/ETCoxford/

[22] Italian dramatist

In October 1941, Flanders made his first major professional appearance on the stage; at the Oxford Playhouse as Mr Valentine the dentist in Shaw's comedy *You Never Can Tell*. He was a lean and long-striding six-foot three, a fine oarsman and quarter-miler and by far the outstanding Oxford actor of his year. His contemporaries had no doubt that he would be the Olivier or Donat of their generation. With his height, athleticism, thin, handsome face, deep intelligence and splendid voice he was formidably, perhaps completely, equipped.[24] His Oxford friend Michael Leversen Meyer wrote that he might have been among the top five actors of his generation.[25] He was going to be in the top class of actors.[26] Incidentally Flanders and Meyer appeared together on television in an episode of *Call My Bluff* in 1968.[27]

He continued to perform at Oxford University and was looking forward to a promising career as an actor when the Navy called him up.[28] So, off he went from Oxford to

---

[23] https://military-history.fandom.com/wiki/Michael_Flanders
[24] Op. cit.
[25] Swann, Donald: Op. cit. p. 133
[26] Amis, John: *Dropping the Hat Again*, Radio 2 documentary, 12th January 1997
[27] https://genome.ch.bbc.co.uk/cd76e01e2ff54ae8895333bc550211e6
[28] http://news.bbc.co.uk/1/hi/magazine/6253824.stm

join the Royal Naval Voluntary Reserve: initially as an Able Seaman.[29]

---

[29] https://dubbing.fandom.com/wiki/Michael_Flanders

CHAPTER TWO
DISASTER; THEN THE EARLY DAYS

Flanders' ship, HMS Marne[30] was torpedoed off the coast of Africa: but he survived. Whilst serving in 1943 as a Sub-Lieutenant on convoys to Russia and Malta he contracted poliomyelitis. He related the story on *Desert Island Discs*.[31] "I was lying off Yarmouth, listening for e-boats - fortunately I never heard one - when I started to feel something that was like a very bad dose of flu; this was eventually diagnosed as polio." One writer commented ironically that Flanders merely contracted polio and with the help of the military's most efficient medical support was condemned to spend the rest of his life in a wheelchair with one lung left completely out of use. Poliomyelitis is a condition which inhibits study at Christ Church – or at least, so Christ Church thought (they could not accommodate cripples).[32] So, Flanders was left

---

[30] On 12th November 1942 a German submarine torpedoed and sunk HMS *Hecla*; minutes later she fired two more torpedoes and badly damaged *Marne*; blowing off her stern

[31] http://news.bbc.co.uk/1/hi/magazine/6253824.stm

[32] Amis, John: *Dropping the Hat Again*, Radio 2 documentary, 12th

trying to become an actor in a world where being disabled was something of a hindrance.[33]

Flanders' commanding officer refused to let him take immediate rest and as a result the polio became far more damaging than it might have been. He spent many months being treated in an iron lung; this had to be specially constructed to fit his long frame. Eventually he was discharged - but his polio meant that he could only walk with great difficulty. After discharge he spent the rest of his life in a wheelchair: and initially he had a rough few years. Overall, he was lucky in that his health was generally good: but Swann reminds us that he had chest problems from time to time: no wonder for all his singing was done on one lung.[34] On top of that - and much later on - he was out of *At the Drop of a Hat* for a month when he caught pneumonia.

Therefore, unable to return to Christ Church to continue his studies, he returned to the family home from which he directed and produced plays with a local amateur theatre group and arranged small musical gatherings with other amateurs including Gerard Hoffnung and Frank Hauser.[35/36]

January 1997
[33] https://thegawain.wordpress.com/2013/03/11/flanders-and-swann/
[34] Swann, Donald: Op. cit. p. 153

As we shall see Flanders found work on the radio - and later in television - and rapidly became a prolific broadcaster making good use of his velvet-brown voice.[37] In addition, he auditioned as a radio actor for the BBC and was considered for the part of the dashing crimefighter Dick Barton (who solved all sorts of crimes and escaped from dangerous situations); however, the BBC said he "did not sound like the voice of an active man:"[38] well they would, wouldn't they.

So, undeterred by his misfortune, Flanders pursued a many-faceted career; performing on stage, concert platforms and screen, making radio broadcasts and recordings. In spite of his disabilities, he became a creative fount. Few men in the theatre can have made so much from a foundation grounded in such misfortune

A chance Oxford reunion in 1948 - the year in which they wrote their first song – was with Donald Swann: at Worcester College Gardens (Swann wearing tortoiseshell glasses and playing the lute in a production of a Greek tragedy).[39] Swann wrote later that it was an historic

---

[35] https://dubbing.fandom.com/wiki/Michael_Flanders
[36] Theatre director who later revitalized the Oxford Playhouse
[37] http://www.donaldswann.co.uk/flanders.html
[38] http://news.bbc.co.uk/1/hi/magazine/6253824.stm
[39] https://www.johnbarber.com/flanders-swann/

moment for them; an answer to prayer.[40] Praise be: he might have been right! Their meeting led to collaboration on several revues directed by Laurier Lister OBE (a contact of Swann: he provided the great breakthrough).[41]/[42]

Now, revues were made up of a string of performers in costume who would perform little acts on a stage with some form of backdrop for scenery. Skits and songs made up the little acts and the audience expected - and were expected - to laugh at the result. Revues were a kind of performance which has largely vanished today: but they were very popular just before and after the War; television killed them.[43] Once they had found some people to let them go professional, the revues including Flanders and Swann were organised by Lister: who Swann described as 'a gentle, devout man.'[44] Later, Lister invited Flanders and Swann to illustrate a talk he was giving at the Bath

---

[40] Swann, Donald: Op. cit. p. 100

[41] George Laurier Lister OBE was an English theatre writer, actor, director and producer. In 1965 he became the first Director of the Yvonne Arnaud Theatre in Guildford. He had a lengthy personal relationship with the Northern Irish actor Max Adrian

[42] Amis, John: *Flanders and Swann,* Radio 2 documentary, 12th January 1997

[43] Amis, John: *Dropping the Hat Again*, BBC documentary, 27th December 1994

[44] Swann, Donald: Op. cit. p. 110

Octagon Chapel.[45] Noting that the audience appreciated their work, they began to work on more numbers.[46]

Flanders and Swann were an unusual act. From this start these two very talented men were to become celebrated. As we shall see, in the 1950s their revue *At the Drop of a Hat* became one of the biggest hit shows. It consisted of two men in dinner suits, a piano and inter alia an audience singing along with the chorus of a song about mud and a hippopotamus.

There was Flanders; bearded and confined to a wheelchair (which one commentator suggested gave him a wonderful air of gravitas).[47] Then again there was Swann at the piano: he had a boyish intellectual look and was referred to by his partner as "an all-round egghead."[48]

A small boy once asked Swann the recipe of his success. He replied "You have to meet someone in a wheelchair who is funny."[49] Swann said of Flanders "He was at once a poet, an actor and a master of a very curious skill: spontaneous improvisation."[50] He continued, saying

---

[45] Until 1890 a Methodist chapel
[46] https://www.johnbarber.com/flanders-swann/
[47] https://www.bbc.co.uk/sounds/play/b00d1025
[48] https://www.johnbarber.com/flanders-swann/
[49] Swann, Donald: Op. cit. p. 174
[50] https://www.johnbarber.com/flanders-swann/

that Flanders made little jokes from everything; and they were carefully noted down;[51] but, he was inclined to call the shots.[52]

Swann explained that they decided on the lyrics at the piano and then composed the music to go with the words.[53] In 1961 Flanders talked to Gordon Snell[54] about the way they wrote; working together at the piano: singing out loud. He said that "writing it down came later."[55] At the end of every day they would play them through to Flanders' mother:[56] at least as a professional violinist she would have appreciated the music!

Of course, prior to the *1968 Theatres Act*,[57] theatre productions were censored. Swann recalled that Roger Lumley (11th Earl of Scarbrough, the Lord Chamberlain) wrote "I like it" when they submitted to him for approval

---

[51] Swann, Donald. Op. cit. p. 133

[52] Amis, John: *Dropping the Hat Again*, Radio 2 documentary, 12th January 1997

[53] Amis, John: Op. cit.

[53] Swann, Donald: Op. cit; p. 149

[54] Born in Singapore: and author and scriptwriter

[55] https://www.bbc.co.uk/sounds/play/b00d1025

[56] Amis, John: sleeve notes for *The Complete Flanders and Swann* CD set

[57] https://www.parliament.uk/about/living-heritage/transformingsociety/private-lives/relationships/collections1/1968-theatre-censorship/1968-theatres-act/

the words of *Smoking is Permitted in the Auditorium'*.[58] Phillips suggested that Flanders and Swann quickly grasped that if the marriage of words and music could be got right, they could produce songs that everyone would want to quote — remembering the tunes or the texts but rarely both — a genuinely popular, cross-discipline and cross-class art form.[59]

1948

In what might have been his radio debut, on Thursday 8th July 1948 at 5.25 p.m. on the Home Service, Flanders was the narrator in the *Railway Children*: which is, of course, one of the most popular stories for both children and adults ever written.

As noted, this was the year in which Flanders first collaborated with Swann. Later, Swann recalled "We wrote our first song. I had gone over to Michael's home near Hampstead Heath to see if he could think of some words for a tune - *In the D'Oyly Cart* [sic] - that I had written". This is an interesting piece. It can seem critical of the way in which the operettas of William Gilbert and

---

[58] Swann, Donald. Op. cit. p. 149
[59] https://www.spectator.co.uk/article/ideal-marriage/

Arthur Sullivan were being performed at this time. Yet it acknowledges the debt owed by Flanders and Swann to Gilbert and Sullivan; leaders of English language musical satire.[60]

This collaboration was accepted by producer Laurier Lister for his new show *Oranges and Lemons* to be staged at the Prince of Wales, the Lyric Theatre Hammersmith and the Globe:[61] among others. There were other compositions by Swann alone in the programme. It was their first joint song and was an obvious Gilbert and Sullivan parody. It was misspelled "D'Oyley" on the album cover; 'Cart' was deliberate. It was first performed in *Oranges and Lemons* with Max Adrian (who Flanders described as "Late and much lamented") as Jack Point, Rose Hill as Yum-Yum and Diana Churchill.[62]

---

[60] https://thegawain.wordpress.com/2013/03/11/flanders-and-swann/

[61] Previously the Hicks Theatre; since 1994 the Gielgud Theatre

[62] http://gasdisc.oakapplepress.com/mdflaswa.htm

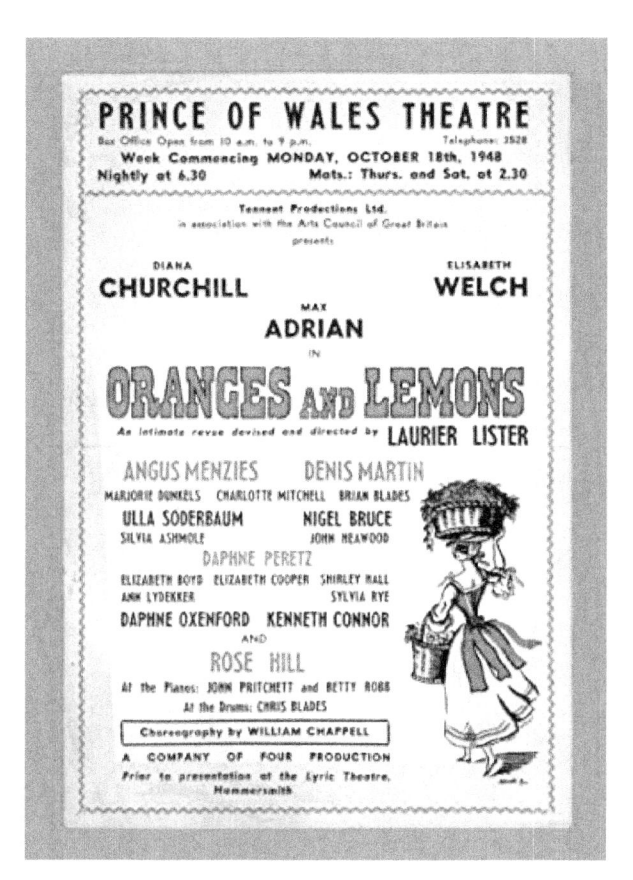

Flyer
Oranges and Lemons

The 4ᵈ Globe programme

Later in the year, on 4th December, Flanders broadcast on the Third Programme at 6.00 p.m. in *Poetry Reading*: it was to be the first of many such broadcasts. He and Robert Marsden[63] read selections from the work of T. S. Eliot and Ezra Pound. Flanders did the same in the programme on 29th December.

1949

Saturday 1st January 1949 Flanders again appeared on the Third Programme in *Poetry Reading* at 11.30 p.m. He and others once more read selections from Eliot and Pound. It was no doubt a programme designed to ease people into sleep. He appeared on the same programme on 3rd February this time reading W. H. Auden, C. Day Lewis, Louis MacNeice, Stephen Spender, Kenneth Allott and George Barker.[64]

Wednesday 12th January at 8.55 p.m. on the Third Programme (it was repeated the next day) Flanders participated in *The Inward Eye* which featured *The Death of a Friend*. A poem by Terence Tiller a shy Cambridge don. He was a Cornish poet who had worked for the

---

[63] He taught Drama at RADA
[64] https://genome.ch.bbc.co.uk/68d9f995028f4c359db2b2f897a99876

BBC Features Department. The programme considered the implications, as felt by a small group of friends, of the death of one of their number in Egypt during WWII.

Saturday 23rd April, the Home Service broadcast *the Life of King Henry V* at 9.15 p.m. Flanders appeared in the chorus.

Flanders early radio broadcast

Tuesday 2nd August at 11.15 p.m. Flanders yet again appeared on the Third Programme at 11.15 p.m. in *W. H. Auden*. He was reading, among others, a selection from *The Sea and the Mirror*: a commentary on Shakespeare's *The Tempest*. Today no one associates Flanders with poetry.

Wednesday 17th August Flanders was on the Third Programme again in *English Satirical Verse* at 10.15 p.m.: an appropriate time for such material. He was one of four readers in a quartet of programmes – this one featuring social satire. The readings were selected by his chum Frank Hauser. (The purpose of satire, it has been said, is to strip away the blanket of comforting illusion and cosy half-truth with which we surround ourselves. Flanders famously once said "Our job, as I see it, is to put it back again").[65]

On Friday 28th October Flanders appeared in *Robert Browning* on the Third Programme at 11.35 p.m. reading *The Patriot* and *Master Hugues of Saxe-Gotha*: this was repeated shortly afterwards.

Later, on Friday 10th November at 10.05 p.m. on the Third Programme, Flanders appeared in *Sir Fulke Greville*. Flanders was one of a number of people who

---

[65] https://tvtropes.org/pmwiki/pmwiki.php/Music/FlandersAndSwann

read extracts from the poetry output[66] of the first Baron Brooke who was granted Warwick Castle by the Crown in 1604.

Saturday 17th December at 4.15 p.m. the Home Service broadcast their *Saturday Matinee* which that week was *The Venus of Bainville* with Flanders as the narrator. Three years later this was made into a television movie.

Oranges and Lemons was highly successful, and Lister commissioned further work. Most of these works were not recorded professionally, though odds and ends found their way through tape recorders onto reel-to-reel tapes. Most were merely retained on paper and a selection emerged later in the album *And Then We Wrote*; this was issued as a celebratory recording for the BBC and released on LP after Flanders' untimely death.[67]

1950

Monday 27th February the Home Service broadcast to schools at 2.00 p.m. Flanders was a narrator for *Stories from World History: Prince Rupert of the Rhine*.[68]

---

[66] Short poems
[67] https://thegawain.wordpress.com/2013/03/11/flanders-and-swann/
[68] How King Charles' nephew (1619-82) and his dog (Boy) became famous during the English Civil War

Tuesday 16th May at 2.15 p.m. on the Home Service Flanders was the narrator of an unknown subject in *For the Schools*.

Monday 4th September (and again on 27th August 1951) on the Light Programme Flanders broadcast in *Hello There!* this was described as a summer holiday magazine. In the first edition Jill Balcon and Flanders invited listeners to inspect their *Poets' Crazy Corner*. Balcon was a long forgotten British actress and the second wife of multi-philanderer Cecil Day Lewis.

Monday 20th November at 6.30 p.m. on the Light Programme, Flanders appeared in *The Younger Generation Under-20 Parade* which was described as a 'slice of life served up for family listening' which this writer imagines had the potential to be terribly tedious. However, Flanders and the record fans (whoever they might have been) argued about mood music.[69]

1951

Friday 9th February, Flanders appeared in a small role in *King Henry VIII* on the Third Programme at 8.40 p.m.

---

[69] Music that is meant to create a relaxed or romantic feeling

The role of Lord Abergavenny was played by Harold Pinter!

On Sunday 11th March at 10.20 p.m. Flanders broadcast on the Third Programme. He was one of two people (along with English actress Rachel Gurney) who read a selection of satirical verse from Jonathan Swift. Twelve days later on Good Friday at 10.20 a.m. Flanders was a contributor in *An Easter I Remember*. One of the co-presenters was Ysanne Churchman (of *Archers* fame: she played Grace Archer who died in the fire in the radio episode broadcast on the night that ITV was launched in 1955).

28th June 1951 *Penny Plain* opened at St Martin's Theatre (now famous for *The Mousetrap)*: Flanders (and Swann) again collaborated on *Prehistoric Complaint* a solo for Max Adrian "dressed in bits of fur as a sort of mis-fit caveman,"[70] This was another revue devised and directed by Laurie Lister. Among many diverse songs, it included Flanders'[71] *Surly Girls* (with Adrian, Desmond Walter-Ellis and Jimmy Thompson; who appeared as a trio of appalling St Trinian's schoolgirls),[72] *Eisteddfod* and *A word in my Ear*.[73] A broadcast on Thursday 12th July at

---

[70] https://military-history.fandom.com/wiki/Michael_Flanders
[71] https://www.antiwarsongs.org/canzone.php?lang=en&id=45084
[72] https://military-history.fandom.com/wiki/Michael_Flanders

7.30 p.m. on the Light Programme featured excerpts from *Penny Plain*[74] which was broadcast again in 1952: their work was gaining a wider audience!

On 14th August at 10.20 p.m., Flanders appeared on the Third Programme - among other contributors - reading a selection of the work of Andrew Marvell: who was an English metaphysical poet in the 17th century.[75] There are not many metaphysical poets around today.

Monday 20th August, Flanders broadcast on *Children's Hour* (One of the all-time most popular radio programmes. Most children growing up after WWII listened to it and have happy memories of it) as narrator of a religious book; *A House to Let* by Mrs. Molesworth.[76]

On Tuesday 28th August on television, Flanders provided a light hearted guide to the subject of *How to be Host*. He introduced some practised guests with hints on hospitality from different parts of the world. His programme appeared at 3.00 p.m. just before *Andy Pandy*

---

[73] https://geneagraphie.com/getperson.php?personID=I364221&tree=1

[74] https://genome.ch.bbc.co.uk/search/0/20?q=Penny+Plain+laurier+lister#top

[75] A group of 17th century English poets whose work was characterised by the inventive use of conceits

[76] Mary Molesworth was an English writer of children's stories who wrote under that name

(for those of you of a certain age): to give you a sense of context.[77]

On Sunday 3rd September at 5.00 p.m., he appeared again as narrator for *Sampo Lappellil* a fairy tale turned into a play by Lucia Turnbull based on a story by Topelius with music by Ianthe Dalway.

---

[77] https://genome.ch.bbc.co.uk/page/402c3132ab124e06bdc761fae7824bac

Penny Plain programme

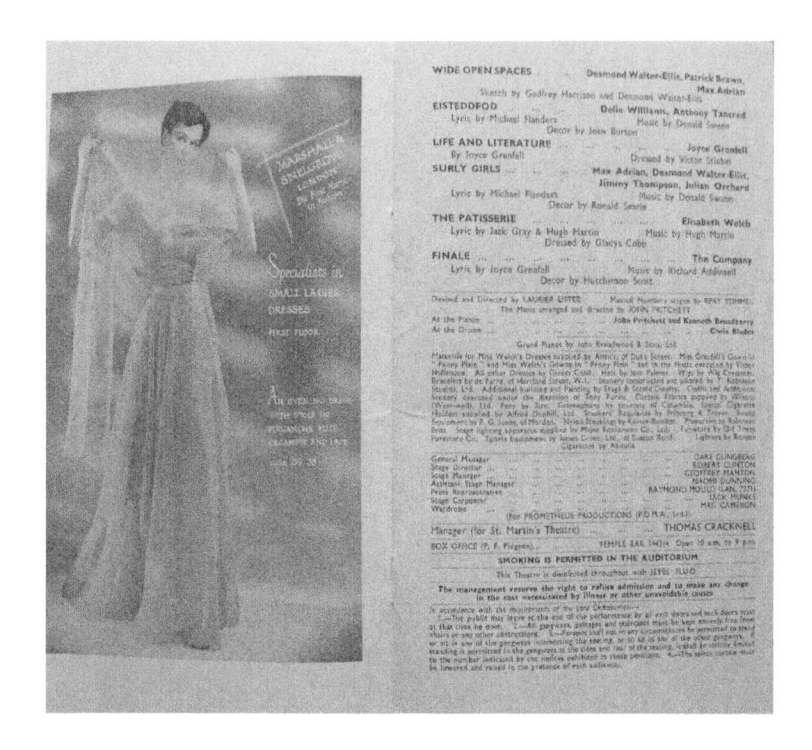

Penny Plain programme continued

Monday 24th September at 7.45 p.m. on the Third Programme Flanders took part in a presentation of Vergil's *Aeneid* as Pyrrhus (Flanders appeared in many other episodes later playing various roles on various dates; he and Douglas Leach[78] were two of several artistes

---

[78] West Country actor

who participated). For those not in the know, this is a Latin epic poem that tells the legendary story of Aeneas who fled the fall of Troy and travelled to Italy where he became the ancestor of the Romans. This is not light reading after you have sunk a few beers.

Once more, he appeared on Saturday 22nd December again as narrator in *Little Red Riding-Hood*. This is usually one of the more horrific of the nursery tales, but Lucia Turnbull had discovered an old version of the tale in which the Wolf is a comic character and the story has a happy ending: as would befit Flanders.

1952

Excerpts from *Penny Plain* (another intimate revue) were broadcast as a television special on Sunday 27th April at 9.30 p.m. with 'lyrics and sketches by Flanders.'[79] [80] Excerpts having previously been broadcast on the radio on Tuesday 29th January at 7.30 p.m.

Penny Plain itself was such a success that Lister invited Flanders and Swann to write much of his next

---

[79] https://genome.ch.bbc.co.uk/schedules/service_bbc_television_service/1952-04-27

[80] https://www.imdb.com/title/tt4641806/?ref_=nm_flmg_wr_6

revue (an intimate revue no less!)[81] *Airs on a Shoestring*. This was staged at the Royal Court Theatre[82] on 22nd April 1953: from where it was broadcast live on 16th July on the Home Service at 8.30 p.m.[83] It was introduced by Brian Johnston. It later toured and was an outstanding success - Berger describes it as their biggest success; running for 772 performances over for two years.[84]

Their topics ranged from economics and politics *(There's a Hole in my Budget)*, a plaintive song about London's last tram *(Last of the Line)* to a send-up of Benjamin Britten's works (*Guide to Britten*).[85]

'Britten' referred to Edward Benjamin Britten OM CH the composer, conductor and pianist who some people consider changed the face of British opera.[86] Britten had formed a close personal relationship with Sir Peter Pears. He was also extremely sensitive to criticism; he often disowned former friends who offended him: which this

---

[81] https://en.wikipedia.org/wiki/Airs_on_a_Shoestring
[82] The *Writers' Theatre*
[83] https://genome.ch.bbc.co.uk/ee204050635147d69f49a43249ff3a6a
[84] https://en.wikipedia.org/wiki/Airs_on_a_Shoestring#:~:text=Airs%20on%20a%20Shoestring%20was,Betty%20Marsden%2C%20and%20Denis%20Quilley.
[85] https://military-history.fandom.com/wiki/Michael_Flanders
[86] https://www.classicfm.com/composers/britten/guides/britten-facts/

writer suspects is why he never went to listen to Flanders' and Swann's work dedicated to him.

Guide to Britten is a straight-up-and-down skit having sly digs at Benjie Britten. It is very demanding both for the audience and for the performers. To appreciate the song the audience needs a fair musical knowledge of Britten's works (such as *The Young Person's Guide to the Orchestra*)[87] to fully enjoy the innuendoes to 1930s singers and references to Pears and Percy Scholes. The piece is huge fun. The pianist gets to winding his stool up and down (*The Turn of the Screw*) and opening and shutting the piano lid. One reviewer said of it "I loved the lines *A Spring Symphony for Sackbut, Psaltry, and Siffleur* and *In America it made Bundles for Britain and Piles for Pears.*"[88]

Saturday 24th May at 3.25 p.m. on the Home Service Flanders appeared in *Storm's Abatement*. Flanders was the storyteller in what was a verse play[89] by Elisabeth Lambert.[90]

---

[87] 1945: an educational piece meant to teach children about all of the different instruments in the orchestra

[88] https://grainger.de/music/songs/guidetobritten.html

[89] Drama written in verse to be performed by an actor before an audience

[90] Elisabeth Lambert Ortiz: an authority on Latin-American and Caribbean cooking: her first book was the verse play *Storm's*

1953

14th June Flanders appeared in *Book in the Shade* on the Light Programme at 3.00 p.m. This was the second of a new series of programmes in which Lionel Gamlin (a teacher turned broadcaster) suggested books for listeners' pleasure and enjoyment; together with readings and dramatic illustrations from those books which were selected.

Christmas Day - and again on Wednesday 30th - Flanders appeared on the Third Programme at 7.40 p.m. in *The Jumblies*[91] *and the Dong;*[92] he was the storyteller in what was a musical entertainment for solo Dong, chorus, and orchestra.

One commentator wrote that 1953 witnessed the arrival of the satirical revue in the shape of *Airs on a Shoestring*. One number, *Sing High, Sing Low* featured a couple. The man was in tails plus white gloves and a gardenia;[93] the woman was a blonde with upswept hair, enormous dangling earrings and a pink crinoline smothered in roses.

Abatement (1949)
[91] https://www.poetryfoundation.org/poems/54364/the-jumblies
[92] A mysterious, fictional figure
[93] Indoor plant, grown for its attractive foliage and highly scented flowers: here, presumably, a button hole

When the couple appeared on stage, they announced "they would sing *Tchaikovsky's Piano Concerto*" – they did not say which one – "arranged as a duet;" the audience fell about.

The 'romantic duettists' then proceeded with their duet, accompanied by kisses, embraces, elaborate gestures and on the final chord, "We detest each other!" The critics approved, finding it had "terrific bite", concerning as it did romantic duettists, no longer young, who sang rubbish and perversions of the classics "just for the dough."[94]

The doyenne of these songs was a little number referred to earlier for three people called *In the D'Oyly Cart*. It was eventually worked into another revue and sung by a trio – none of whom were Flanders or Swann.[95] For the next eight years together the two wrote substantial portions of half a dozen major West End revues.[96] Flanders remarked "We complement each other"[97] which was something of an understatement. Swann remarked that, although he composed items with a number of other

---

[94] https://theatricalia.com/play/3y3/airs-on-a-shoestring/production/8jd
[95] https://thegawain.wordpress.com/2013/03/11/flanders-and-swann/
[96] http://www.donaldswann.co.uk/flanders.html
[97] https://soundcloud.com/nfsaaustralia/flanders-and-swann-interviewed

people at that time, every work that he completed with Flanders was "always snapped up."[98]

Graham McCann thought Flanders and Swann "the most influential British double act in comedy," ahead of Morecambe and Wise, the Two Ronnies *and* Peter Cook and Dudley Moore. He wrote "Michael Flanders and Donald Swann have had a profound and lasting impact not only on British comedy and music, but also on just about every other major point and place in the panorama of British entertainment over the last sixty years." In the spirit of the time, Flanders commented "We are genial old men rather than angry young men."[99] Writing in 2021, McCann continued "the sad thing is: it's sort of a secret. Flanders and Swann just do not get mentioned much these days."[100]

---

[98] Swann, Op. cit p. 21
[99] https://www.bbc.co.uk/sounds/play/b00d1025
[100] https://www.comedy.co.uk/features/comedy_chronicles/remarkable-legacy-of-flanders-and-swann/

Airs on a Shoestring programme

1954

Wednesday 1st September at 10.10 p.m. television broadcast *Three's Company*.[101] This was an improbable opera. The libretto[102] was written by Flanders.[103] The story relates that Mr Love's father left his business to his son and to Mr Three, his senior clerk. Mr Three, an efficient businessman, is in charge until the naive and inefficient Mr Love develops more business acumen. The bewitching Miss Honey is engaged as a new secretary and Mr Love immediately falls for her. Mr Three, not to be outdone, uses his prosperity and senior position to turn the tables and Miss Honey and he go off for a 'trial' week together, leaving a suicidal Mr Love behind. This time, however, Mr Three has bitten off more than he can chew and on his return he too is suicidal. It emerges that profits have doubled during Mr Three's absence, so Mr Love, who has done nothing, stakes his claim to seniority and Miss Honey reverts to her first man.[104] This was later broadcast

---

[101] https://genome.ch.bbc.co.uk/b7ffed1de25d4c578c0ee46af7bb3b08
[102] The text of an opera
[103] Composer and writer Antony Hopkins wrote the music
[104] https://www.wisemusicclassical.com/work/35282/Threes-Company--Antony-Hopkins/

on radio on Thursday 21st March 1957[105] on the Home Service.

In September 1954 in collaboration with Kitty Black,[106] Flanders translated Stravinsky's *The Soldier's Tale*[107] for the Edinburgh Festival at the King's Theatre. Based on a Russian folk tale, the piece (written to be spoken, played and danced) tells the story of a Russian soldier who is returning home on leave when he encounters the Devil disguised as an old man. He convinces the soldier to trade his fiddle for a book predicting the future.

When Joseph finally returns home, he learns that he has been gone for three years. Believing him dead, his fiancé has married another man. Although the soldier acquires great wealth, he loses everything that makes life worthwhile, including the ability to play the fiddle. Moving to another country, he learns that the King's daughter is ill, and her hand in marriage has been offered to anyone who cures her. Joseph wins back his fiddle, recovers his musical ability and revives the Princess.

Wednesday 14th October (and again in November and January 1955) Flanders appeared on the Light Programme at 6.15 p.m. on the *Younger Generation Presents Review*:

---

[105] And again, on 1st November 1954
[106] South African playwright/translator
[107] As the standard translation it has been recorded many times

in which young people discussed current films, books, plays and tunes. There was a great fad in the 1950s for soliciting the views of young people on almost every topic: rather as though they were a newly discovered breed. The programme also featured Fun and Frolic – which must have been diabolical. Flanders gave the results of the previous week's competition and set another one. Later, it became apparent that he obviously had a thing about setting competitions.

14th November the Third Programme broadcast *Emily Butter: an Occasion Recalled* for which the music was composed by Swann. This was the third of Henry Reed's[108] radio plays about an imaginary writer Richard Shewin.[109] Shewin's friend (the 'lady music writer' Hilda Tablet[110]) only played a small part in the first play but by the third had an entire operatic premiere devoted to her. Flanders was one of two male commentators. A new production was broadcast in February 1958 and on 30th March 1962. It was repeated in June 1987.

Saturday 11th December - and again six days later - Flanders was a guest on *The Younger Generation Family Circle* in which the youth invited the older generation to

---

[108] British poet, dramatist and journalist
[109] https://audiodrama.fandom.com/wiki/Emily_Butter
[110] Fictional creator of reinforced concrete music

join in listening to some of the highlights of the week's programmes and to meet Flanders; the guest of the week.

Flanders wrote the libretto for *Christmas Story* which was broadcast on television on Monday 20th December at 9.45 p.m. This was presented by the *Intimate Opera Company*. Alas, it was televised but never published or recorded.

The action took place in a bedroom during the early hours of Christmas morning. It had been a long day and Mother wanted to go to sleep. Father, dressed as Santa Claus, was all set to take the children their presents in the adjoining nursery. It was 3.00 a.m. and there was a burglar about. He too was seasonably dressed as Santa Claus! All the scene required now was the real Santa Claus to confuse and confound the others.

An EP of the same name - *Christmas Story* (and not to be confused with the television programme) - was issued later in 1959 on Parlophone.

Flanders and Swann wrote the songs for *Pay the Piper*. A revue at the Saville Theatre[111] which opened on 21st December ~~~~ and which alas closed on the 8th January 1955: so, it was obviously a bit of a bummer. Swann says

---

[111] Now converted into the four-screen Odeon Cinema, Covent Garden

that the show was "a complex revue" and attracted a "severe lack of audiences."[112] Interestingly, the cast included Elsie and Doris Waters who were big hitters at that time and were sisters of Jack Warner the actor who played Dixon of Dock Green.[113]

---

[112] Swann, Donald: Op. cit. p. 121
[113] https://www.guidetomusicaltheatre.com/shows_p/paypiper.htm

Pay the Piper

1955

Wednesday 30th March on the Light Programme at 6.15 p.m. Flanders appeared in the *Younger Generation Review Forum*. With an audience of young film making and stagecraft amateurs, the panel discussed - and answered question about - the place of the amateur in show business.

Wednesday 29th June Flanders broadcast on the Third Programme at 6.55 p.m. in *Orestes*;[114] in an English version by Ary van Nierop and Flanders. It was a radiophonic opera devised and composed by Henk Badings;[115] Flanders played the spoken part of Pylades.[116]

---

[114] Greek mythology: Orestes was the son of Clytemnestra and Agamemnon and brother of Electra. There are several Ancient Greek plays connected with his madness and purification

[115] Dutch composer, best known for his music featuring electronic sounds

[116] Pylades was Orestes' cousin and (and possibly homoerotic) close friend

Orestes on the Third Programme

3rd July, 10th and the 17th (on the latter two occasions with Julian Bream), Flanders appeared in *Sunday in Summer* on the Light Programme at 9.10 a.m. in a morning miscellany.[117] If you will excuse the black pun, by this time he was truly finding his feet in radio

---

[117] https://genome.ch.bbc.co.uk/schedules/service_light_programme/1955-07-03

broadcasting: and it was to lead him to a lifelong career in the genre.

Sunday in Summer
on the Light Programme

Next, Flanders appeared in a BP documentary *The New Explorers*. This looked into aspects of the life and work of those who seek oil for tomorrow's needs. It consisted of six episodes showing various aspects of British Petroleum's search for oil - negotiations with a sheik in the Persian Gulf, rock-sampling in Canada, dynamiting in Zanzibar, pioneering in Papua, drilling the sea-bed off Trinidad and well-testing in Sicily. In no case is oil actually found (the odds are 6-1 against). In each location a different aspect of the story of the search for oil unfolded. It featured a calypso written by Flanders himself.[118]

On Thursday 3rd November (and further editions in early 1956) Flanders broadcast on the Light Programme at 6.30 p.m. in *All Yours!* In the first programme the participants discussed good books that they had read recently and Flanders set a Younger Generation competition. In one programme listeners under twenty-one were asked to compose a poem, short story, or article with the title *The Sea*. On Thursday 8th December Flanders was again in the chair and he set both that week's competition and the special Christmas one. In the first January programme he featured the winning entries of his open competition subject: *Seven*.[119/120]

---

[118] http://www.screenonline.org.uk/film/id/1351308/credits.html

[119] https://genome.ch.bbc.co.uk/page/835360396de2402e8a67022be91ee2da

[120] https://genome.ch.bbc.co.uk/9551315bd3a24764abc21c0d2e3d034d

Friday 18th November Flanders appeared in *Parade* on the Light Programme at 7.30 p.m. This was a programme for family listening once again presented by members of the Younger Generation. Flanders was creating a niche for himself broadcasting to a younger audience. In this edition young people from the Stepney Jewish Senior Club, in the throes of rehearsing their own show, met three experts on the subject: Flanders, William Chappell[121] and Ian Carmichael. Ten months later in another edition the programme featured Mary Duddy who had become a pupil of Britain's first regular water ski-ing school at Poole and Don Durbridge who questioned the American bandleader Bill Haley on the origin and future of Rock 'n' Roll - which thanks to Tommy Steele - had just taken the UK by storm.

Wednesday 28th December at 3.00 p.m. on the Light Programme - and in later editions - the BBC broadcast *Holiday Hamper*: a surprise basket of entertainment which was unpacked by Flanders with the help of Elton Hayes, Donald Swann, Benjamin Kennard, John Kruse and the Kukaburra Bird. It proved to be a surprise assortment for fifteens and under.

---

[121] He was an English writer on music *and* a partner in the musical firm Chappell & Co

Our narrative, now takes an important change of direction. Flanders and Swann had first performed their own work together in *Private View* on 1ˢᵗ December[122] in 1950 at Whistler's[123] Ballroom on Cheyne Walk.[124] Swann described this as a key point in their relationship.[125] They invited some of their friends along to listen. Ian Wallis, John Schlesinger and Peter Ustinov were among those who turned up. Swann said in 1993 that those who were there still remembered it. Flanders was exemplary but no one thought that a man in a wheelchair would go on stage. But he did and, as a result, he began to believe in himself as a performer.[126]

In fact, over time, he made the wheelchair part of the act and clumped around in it and lifted it up and thumped it down. He performed one song about the sea and he made the wheelchair roll around as though it was on the ocean.[127]

---

[122] Berger, Leon: *Hat-Tricks: guide to the songs*
[123] American born artist James McNeill Whistler lived at 96 Cheyne Walk
[124] https://www.filmedlivemusicals.com/drop-another-hat.html
[125] Swann, Donald: Op. cit. p. 121
[125] Op. cit. p. 123
[126] Op. cit. p. 124
[127] https://www.bbc.co.uk/sounds/play/b00d1025

1956

> **ROYAL FESTIVAL HALL**
> General Manager T. E. Bean
>
> TUESDAY, JUNE 5 at 10.45 p.m.
>
> LATE NIGHT CONCERT
>
> The L.C.C. in association with the Institute of Contemporary Arts (British Section of I.S.C.M.)
>
> presents
>
> # The SOLDIER'S TALE
>
> IGOR STRAVINSKY
>
> A CONCERT PERFORMANCE WITH
>
> Sir RALPH RICHARDSON — The Soldier
> PETER USTINOV — The Devil
> MICHAEL FLANDERS — Narrator
>
> CHAMBER ENSEMBLE led by Manoug Parikian
> FRANCIS BAINES (Double Bass)   HAROLD JACKSON (Trumpet)
> JACK BRYMER (Clarinet)   SIDNEY LANGSTON (Trombone)
> ARCHIE CAMDEN (Bassoon)   STEPHEN WHITTAKER (Percussion)
>
> **ALEXANDER GIBSON** conductor
>
> TICKETS: 5/- unreserved, from the ROYAL FESTIVAL HALL BOX OFFICE (WATerloo 3191) and usual agents
> The concert is expected to finish at approximately 11.40 p.m.
> For the convenience of patrons, the buffet will be open before the concert

The Soldier's Tale
Royal Festival Hall flyer

Once more, The *Soldier's Tale* played to a capacity audience. This time in London at the Royal Festival Hall on 5th June with Flanders as the narrator. The translation has held its place into the 21st century as the standard English version.[128]

Swann moved in with Flanders to his flat at Number One, Scarsdale Villas, South Kensington for a short while.[129] Quite a number of interesting people had lived in the Villas over time: it was Flanders' problems with getting safely out of his car outside Number One (and while in a wheelchair) that was the basis for his introduction to his famous song *The Gnu*. Swann remarked that the flat was commodious and that Flanders was able to whizz around happily in his wheelchair.[130] Incidentally, Flanders caused the pronunciation of gnu (g-nu) to be changed in perpetuity.[131] In the song he refers to Rustington-on-Sea: now just *Rustington* this is a resort in West Sussex.

---

[128] https://military-history.fandom.com/wiki/Michael_Flanders
[129] Value today £6,500,000
[130] Swann, Donald. Op. cit. p. 124
[131] Amis, John: sleeve notes for *The Complete Flanders and Swann* CD set

Number 1 Scarsdale Villas

the number of the car pictured is not GNU

Now; classical music critic John Amis was famous for his Summer School of Music[132] which had begun at Bryanston School in 1948.[133] In 1953 it moved to Dartington Hall, Totnes. By 1956, Flanders and Swann were sufficiently established to be invited to give a lecture on writing revue songs.[134] Swann felt that taking everything into account Flanders could cope with getting around in his wheelchair.[135] Amis invited them to do a cabaret on the last night of the week and Swann recalls that they were billed as *An Evening with Michael Flanders and Donald Swann.*[136] This was an historic moment!

The pair were a wow - the audience clamoured for more[137] - and the very fact that they were appreciated by a discriminating audience gave them confidence. It was here that Flanders started his practice of introducing each song with a short narrative. This seemed to be as popular with the audience as were the songs themselves and it

---

[132] Then three weeks - now four - of shared music from early music to jazz: shared music making and listening

[133] https://www.dartington.org/john-amis/

[134] Introduced 1953

[135] Swann, Donald. Op. cit. p. 125

[136] Op. cit. p. 125

[137] Amis, John: sleeve notes for *The Complete Flanders and Swann* CD set

became a regular part of the act:[138] indeed perhaps almost Flanders' trademark. One wonders what gave him the inspiration. This writer also believes that it was the act's *Unique Selling Point* and quite simply made the show. Amis comments that Flanders' patter changed – as time went on – adapting to changing events and indeed his whim of the moment.[139]

In the same year, Flanders and Swann were involved with *Fresh Airs* ('A revue by Michael Flanders and Donald Swann')[140] which was staged in Brighton and London. It opened on the 26th January at the Comedy Theatre[141] again directed by Laurier Lister.[142] It was the last in Lister's series of '*Airs*'; the revues before Flanders and Swann went off on their own.[143] Several of the songs that Flanders and Swann used for *encores* in their shows originated from this production.

---

[138] https://h2g2.com/entry/A658857
[139] Amis, John: sleeve notes for *The Complete Flanders and Swann* CD set
[140] http://www.guidetomusicaltheatre.com/shows_f/freshairs.htm
[141] Now the *Harold Pinter Theatre*
[142] https://ovrtur.com/production/2891173
[143] https://en.wikipedia.org/wiki/Fresh_Airs

AT THE DOFF OF A HAT

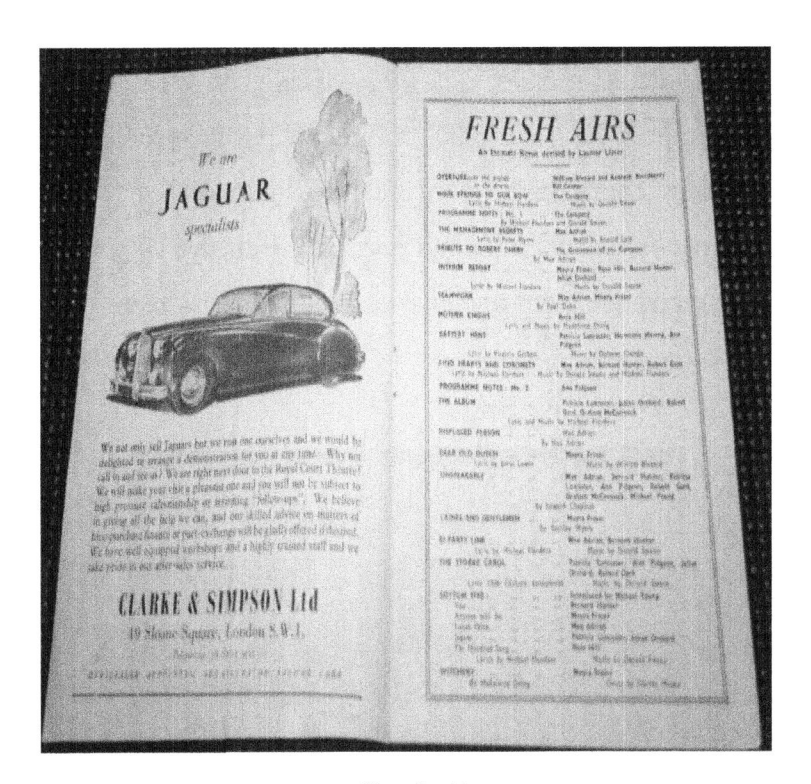

Fresh Airs
London programme

Sunday 21st October, Flanders appeared as Chairman on *Anglo-American Question Time* on the Light Programme at 4.30 p.m. It would have appealed to Flanders enormously as it featured a team of young American students who had just arrived in the UK. They exchanged questions and answers with a British team.

Anglo American Relations

On 11th November Flanders appeared in *Question Time* on the Light Programme at 4.30 p.m. He was in the chair (both literally and metaphorically) in a programme in which a group of young people from all around the world put questions on the colour problem to four people who are now long forgotten!

Two days later, on Tuesday 13th November at 8.05 p.m. Flanders was commentator at the (first of three) *Hoffnung Music Festival Concerts*.[144/145] These were humorous classical music festivals. The BBC had visited the Royal Festival Hall to record part of what proved to be a series of most unusual musical occasions: it would have been right up Flanders' street.

On Boxing Day, Flanders appeared on the Home Service at 6.25 p.m. in a programme for listeners in the South East entitled *Town and Country*: his contribution being a story and song: and we know nothing of either.

---

[144] Released on record by Columbia
[145] There were further concerts in 1958 and 1961

CHAPTER THREE
INTO THE UNKNOWN

It was not until 1956 that Flanders and Swann decided to write and perform their own full stage show. The unlikely pairing of the bearded, wheelchair-bound Flanders and the bespectacled, aesthete Swann produced one of those happy partnerships of opposites. Swann wrote the music; Flanders the words; both "for want of a better word" sang.[146]

Flanders wrote songs 'with a message:'[147] and in his own mind was the 'actor and director';[148] which if you think it about it rationally made perfectly good sense. Swann recalls that he and Flanders were establishing a new genre: that of 'author performers': best of all, people were loving it![149] Indeed Amis suggests that their production defied description; it was, he suggested, *sui generis* (one of a kind).[150]

---

[146] https://h2g2.com/entry/A658857
[147] Amis, John: BBC documentary, 27th December 1994
[148] Swann, Donald: Op. cit. p. 184
[149] Op. cit, p. 130

The title of their wacky revue *At the Drop of a Hat* evolved from Flanders' and Swann's readiness, at any gatherings of friends, to perform their collaborations;[151] and to do so spontaneously, ad hoc.[152] Their performances went down so well[153] that they decided to take the plunge and to appear on a stage.

Flanders was reportedly nervous about performing in a wheelchair;[154] but, of course, as we have seen the wheelchair morphed into a stage prop;[155] indeed such a successful one that he was the first wheelchair user to perform with the Royal Shakespeare Company.[156] Indeed, he advanced the cause of the disabled by lobbying - and by example - and possessed the remarkable skill of putting others at ease about his predicament whatever his immense personal difficulties.[157]

So, it came about that Amis suggested that they went to a theatre. Swann says that they mailed all those who had

---

[150] Amis, John: sleeve notes for *The Complete Flanders and Swann* CD set
[151] https://www.nytimes.com/1975/04/16/archives/michael-flanders-is-dead-at-53-humoriststar-of-drop-of-a-hat.html
[152] For a specific purpose, problem or task
[153] http://news.bbc.co.uk/1/hi/magazine/6253824.stm
[154] https://www.filmedlivemusicals.com/drop-another-hat.html
[155] Amis, John: BBC documentary, 27th December 1994
[156] https://flandersandswann.info/originals/
[157] http://www.donaldswann.co.uk/flanders.html

given them such a good response at Dartington and those enthusiasts provided them with their first audience.[158]

So, the stage was set; literally! The New Lindsey Theatre (a small intimate theatre which, alas, is now a car park)[159] was available until 21st January 1957 when *The Chicken Play* was due to open.[160] Flanders and Swann could hire it for £40 a week. Berger relates the story that Flanders and Swann invited the manager of the theatre to visit them in Flanders' studio. Freddie Piffard heard their material and said "You pay the rent; it's up to you."[161]

So, they hired the New Lindsey Theatre Club,[162] an out of the way fringe theatre[163] (seating capacity 150) at Palace Gardens Terrace, Notting Hill Gate for a three-week run ending on 20th January 1957.

---

[158] Swann, Donald. Op cit. p. 126

[159] https://www.johnbarber.com/flanders-swann/

[160] Amis, John: sleeve notes for *The Complete Flanders and Swann* CD set

[161] Berger, Leon: *Hat-Tricks: guide to the songs*

[162] Established as the Lindsey Theatre Club on 19th March 1940

[163] https://books.google.co.uk/books?id=oWLRDwAAQBAJ&pg=PA11&lpg=PA11&dq=at+the+drop+of+a+hat+flanders+and+swann&source=bl&ots=yYJsA3QnAM&sig=ACfU3U1HI3c5Dhk_k7Gi61pH72iUEGduVw&hl=en&sa=X&ved=2ahUKEwjS3q7Lv5r9AhX7REEAHbrmCCU4RhDoAXoECAQQAw#v=onepage&q=at%20the%20drop%20of%20a%20hat%20flanders%20and%20swann&f=false

The New Lindsey was no more than a large cellar, reached by narrow stairs. On arrival, you had to fight your way through a crowd of serious drinkers arranged around the pool table.[164] Alas within twelve months this *historic!* building had been demolished as part of a road widening scheme![165]

Flanders and Swann opened on New Year's Eve 1956, with a show which they referred to as "An After-Dinner Farrago."[166] Amis says they claimed to have invented the word themselves: but he never disillusioned them because he knew that the word derived from the Latin word for *corn*: although it has morphed into meaning *medley*.[167]

The poster proclaimed that in *At the Drop of a Hat* Flanders and Swann would perform regardless. Top priced seats were 10/6^d. The show began at 8 o'clock; potential patrons were asked to note, 'Bicycles at 10'![168] It was a musical without scenery, with two grey curtains as a backdrop and a cast that admitted to hiring their suits from Moss Bros.[169]

---

[164] https://www.3ammagazine.com/3am/lord-of-junk-himself/
[165] https://flandersandswann.info/originals/
[166] i.e, a *hotchpotch. Nonsense and muddle*
[167] Amis, John: sleeve notes for *The Complete Flanders and Swann* CD set
[168] http://briansibleysblog.blogspot.com/2008/02/who-says-nostalgia-isnt-what-it-was.html

As at Dartington earlier, Flanders wrote a script linking the songs and realized almost immediately that his text was getting more laughs than the songs themselves.[170] The strength of this technique was that Flanders would invent all sorts of strange funny lines: and Swann would laugh about one second before the audience: as a result of this original technique, the show became a new experience almost every night.[171]

When Flanders and Swann decided to perform their own material, it was Flanders' first professional appearance on the stage since contracting polio. He introduced himself as "The big one with the beard who writes all the words and does most of the talking". Years later, Flanders jokingly told Binny Lum[172] that he was mistaken for Father Christmas from time to time. In the same interview he jokingly told Lum that Swann was not a very good pianist: but, he said, "His laugh is so wonderful."

Several critics came and raved about the show. Flanders' old school friend Anthony Wedgewood Benn

---

[169] https://www.johnbarber.com/flanders-swann/
[170] Swann, Donald. Op cit. p. 127
[171] Op. cit. p. 132
[172] https://soundcloud.com/nfsaaustralia/flanders-and-swann-interviewed

opined that the whole thing appealed to every age group[173] for it was a very sharp social commentary without malice.

Flanders could not believe that an audience was watching him in a wheelchair. Joyce Grenfell[174] said "You must go on tour." It was she who loved to sing their *Song of the Weather*: but felt compelled to change the last line.[175] Two weeks into the run they agreed to stay on for a third week.[176] It was by all accounts a remarkable performance. There was a bare stage, Flanders was at one side, Swann seated at the piano at the other - and the only prop was a standard lamp; yet they brought the house down night after night.[177]

The press notices were good. Audiences were sparse on days two and three[178] but thereafter the box-office did excellent business: next the pair were offered a West End transfer. Jack Minster and E.P. Clift had the lease on the Fortune theatre and told them that they should transfer there at once.[179] Swann recalled in 1977, "We turned it

---

[173] Amiss, John: *Dropping the Hat Again*, Radio 2 documentary, 12th January 1997

[174] Very well-known English *diseuse*

[175] Berger, Leon: *Hat-Tricks: guide to the songs*

[176] Swann, Donald. Op cit. p. 128

[177] https://h2g2.com/entry/A658857

[178] Amis, John: sleeve notes for *The Complete Flanders and Swann* CD set

[179] Swann, Donald. Op cit. p. 128

down unanimously. It seemed to spell the end of Flanders' radio career (he had by that time done at least a thousand broadcasts) and the end of Swann as composer."[180] It is amazing to consider that Flanders had achieved so many radio broadcasts since beginning work after his illness.

---

[180] https://military-history.fandom.com/wiki/Michael_Flanders

THE NEW LINDSEY THEATRE CLUB
NOTTING HILL GATE

★

From

New Year's Eve

FOR A SHORT SEASON

At the drop of a hat —

MICHAEL FLANDERS
&
DONALD SWANN

AUTHORS OF *AIRS ON A SHOESTRING* - *FRESH AIRS*
WALLACE'S PRIVATE ZOO etc.

will perform - regardless

TUES. TO SAT. AT 8 – SUN. AT 5 & 8
BOX-OFFICE: BAYSWATER 2512 - 11 TO 7.30 SUN. FROM 3.30
SEATS: 10/6 7/6 5/- 3/6

Bicycles at 1/0

A historic notice

So, the production transferred on the 24th January 1957 to the intimate Fortune Theatre in Covent Garden, where it ran for nearly two and a half years: it was a manager's dream because there were virtually no overheads: it was just two men and a piano on a stage.[181] Swann said that the theatre was not very clean at the start of their run and some seats collapsed during one of their early shows: a whole row of people just faded out.[182]

The production opened to great acclaim and ran for 759 performances. Enthusiasts included the Royal Family, almost all of whom were reported to have been heard singing along to *Mud, Mud, Glorious Mud*.[183] Swann remarked that very soon after they opened the makeup of the audience changed from their old Dartington supporters to great swathes of the general public.[184]

---

[181] Swann, Donald. Op. cit. p. 131
[182] Op. cit. p. 129
[183] https://www.filmedlivemusicals.com/blog/up-close-with-flanders-swann
[184] Op. cit. p. 131

1957

The beloved
Fortune Theatre, Covent Garden

At the drop of a Hat
MICHAEL FLANDERS and DONALD SWANN
(Recorded during an actual performance at the Fortune Theatre, London)

21st February 1957

First recording – Parlophone PMC1033

Flanders' and Swann's very first disc!

US *Variety* magazine reported on 30th January that the show succeeded as an offbeat entertainment and did so mainly on the quality of Flanders' lines and his outstanding personality: 'an unlikely prospect for the West End: a show strictly for the chi-chi[185] trade'. It reported his faultless delivery and shrewd wit.[186] Anthony

---

[185] Stylish elegance
[186] https://lantern.mediahist.org/catalog/variety205-1957-01_0588

Wedgewood Benn saw them as cartoonists: but with the medium being music.[187]

Within twenty-eight days of opening, George Martin[188] of Parlophone had arranged a mono recording of the show and released it as a long-playing record – much cut down and with one or two songs missing from the original performance. It was released in New Zealand, Australia and South Africa: as well as in North America on the Angel label.[189]

All the while, Flanders kept in touch with other activities. *What's My Line* was one of the most popular quiz shows of the 1950s and made people like Lady Barnett[190] famous. It was based on the US game show of the same name and aired on television from 1951 to 1963. The object of the game was to guess the job of the person being interviewed based upon given clues. Flanders appeared as a panellist on the 10th February 1957; along with Isobel Barnett, Jean Dawnay[191] and Bob Monkhouse.

Tuesday 23rd April at 9.00 p.m. on the Light Programme Flanders was the Celebrity Choice on

---

[187] https://www.bbc.co.uk/sounds/play/b00d1025
[188] Later Sir George
[189] https://www.discogs.com/release/5400766-Michael-Flanders-And-Donald-Swann-At-The-Drop-Of-A-Hat-An-After-Dinner-Farrago
[190] An elegant and witty Scottish doctor
[191] Fame is transient: she was a British fashion model

Tuesday Tune Time which provided music in all directions!

Meanwhile, Flanders and Swann had become an established triumph with *At the Drop of a Hat*. It made them both famous and they received over two hundred offers to appear in cabaret.[192] The BBC broadcast *Theatre Flash: from At the Drop of a Hat* on Monday 31st on television at 9.45 p.m.

On 17th June and again on the 8th July Flanders and Swann - described as the men of the moment[193] - broadcast on *Passing Parade* at 8.15 p.m. on the Home Service. This was a weekly magazine programme and included among others Bill Kerr who had made his name on *Hancock's Half Hour*.

The following month, Flanders appeared on *I'll never forget the day* on Tuesday 9th July at 4.15 p.m. on the Home Service. He made a good joke by singing *I'll never forget the day; the day I met my mother*. In reality his appearance was deadly serious for he discussed how he remembered the day in November 1943 when he had a headache. This was, of course, the ailment that ended up with his spending the rest of his life in a wheelchair.

---

[192] Swann, Donald. Op. cit. p. 135

[193] https://genome.ch.bbc.co.uk/dd1b671d25fd48d092771cd7fd23fb66

Theatre Flash

The 12th July saw Flanders and Swann at the famous Abbey Road studios recording their *More Out Of The Hat* EP for Parlophone.[194] This featured a handful of songs featured in the show but omitted from the original LP.

Saturday 31st August *The Hunting of the Snark*[195] was broadcast on the Third Programme at 11.00 p.m. Composed by Max Saunders and with an orchestra conducted by Clifton Helliwell, this was a musical version of the famous nonsense poem composed for broadcasting

On Friday 6th September Flanders and Swann appeared on *Edmundo Ros* on television at 6.45 p.m. featuring the star of the same name with whom the host did some musical research (a description which is open to any interpretation). Ros was a well-known Trinidadian-Venezuelan musician, vocalist and arranger; but he was best known as a bandleader.

Tuesday 29th October at 8.35 p.m. on the Third Programme Flanders was one of two translators in yet another production of Stravinsky's *Soldier's Tale*. This was the first of six programmes to mark the great Russian composer's seventy-fifth birthday.

---

[194] Berger, Leon: *Hat-Tricks: guide to the songs*
[195] Subtitled *An Agony in 8 Fits*, this is a nonsense poem by Lewis Carrol

Then on Sunday 8th December at 7.30 p.m., excerpts from *At the Drop of a Hat*, along with excerpts from *The Boyfriend*, were aired on Alan Melville's *On Stage - London*, a television show that featured excerpts of current British stage hits.[196] Melville was a broadcaster and raconteur: and early television star: one who was very smooth, urbane and sophisticated.

---

[196] https://www.filmedlivemusicals.com/at-the-drop-hat.html

AT THE DOFF OF A HAT

On-Stage - London

1958

In January - by which time this writer had actually seen Flanders and Swann in the flesh - *The Times* commented[197] 'it does something to explain the continued popularity of their two-man revue that Flanders and Swann did not mark the significance of yesterday evening's show (being its first anniversary in the West End) until they had gone right through the performance, ensuring its success; like that of any previous show during the run, entirely on its own merits. The paper continued they 'made no concession to their anniversary until a second encore was requested after the statutory nineteen items. With Mr. Swann's piano as the only accessory to the exercise of their joint inventiveness *and* with each of them, by being and remaining himself, the one offsets the other beautifully.'

Sunday 9th March Flanders appeared on the Home Service at 9.10 a.m. in *Home for the Day*; Marjorie Anderson[198] (of blessed memory) introduced Flanders who had recently been her guest on *Woman's Hour*.

---

[197] The Times, London, January 1957
[198] Marjorie Anderson MBE was a British actress and radio broadcaster for over thirty years: she presented *Woman's Hour* from 1958 to 1972

Meanwhile, the *Brains Trust* was introduced by the BBC originally to provide more serious programmes for the Forces radio service.[199] At its peak, this hugely popular radio show was listened to by up to 29% of the population and received around 4400 letters per week.[200]

It was adapted by producer Howard Thomas from the American programme *Information Please*: and it was he who coined the term *Question Master*. The panel were not briefed on the questions: some of their answers gave rise to catchphrases, such as Joad's[201] qualifying "It all depends what you mean by ..." Questions ranged from the trivial to the serious, for example "Do we think this world is worthwhile?" *The Brains Trust* continued until 1949 with many eminent brains, before transferring to television in 1950. Flanders was the Question Master (and once as a panellist) for nineteen televised episodes between 1958 and 1959.[202] His first appearance was on Sunday 27th April at 4.15 p.m. The now erudite Flanders said that he

---

[199] Wartime radio station for forces overseas
[200] https://www.npg.org.uk/collections/search/person-list.php?grp=1323&displayNo=60
[201] English intellectual and broadcaster. He appeared on *The Brains Trust* and popularised philosophy. He became a celebrity, before his downfall in a scandal over an unpaid train fare in 1948
[202] https://www.imdb.com/title/tt0276652/fullcredits?ref_=tt_ov_st_sm

preferred performing to writing and that he wrote mainly "to give myself something to perform:" which was a transparently sensible observation.

We now come to *Studio 'E'*. This was a television magazine programme for older children (it was a forerunner to *Blue Peter*) that ran for three years from 7th January 1957[203] and was broadcast from 5.00 p.m. to 6.00 p.m. It featured a general mix of entertainment and educational material suitable for older children. Flanders and Swann appeared on the show on Monday 12th May[204] 'with some of their songs': and it would undoubtedly have required no acting on their part whatsoever.

Saturday 17th May at 8.00 p.m. on the Home Service the BBC broadcast *Toast of the Town*. Needless to say, as they were indeed the toast of London, Flanders and Swann were paid a sparkling tribute (450 performances and still running) by Eamonn Andrews; as outstanding newcomers and successes in the world of London entertainment.

---

[203] https://w.televisionheaven.co.uk/reviews/studio-e

[204] https://genome.ch.bbc.co.uk/page/7b71561ba86e4b9b9011c4a677626540

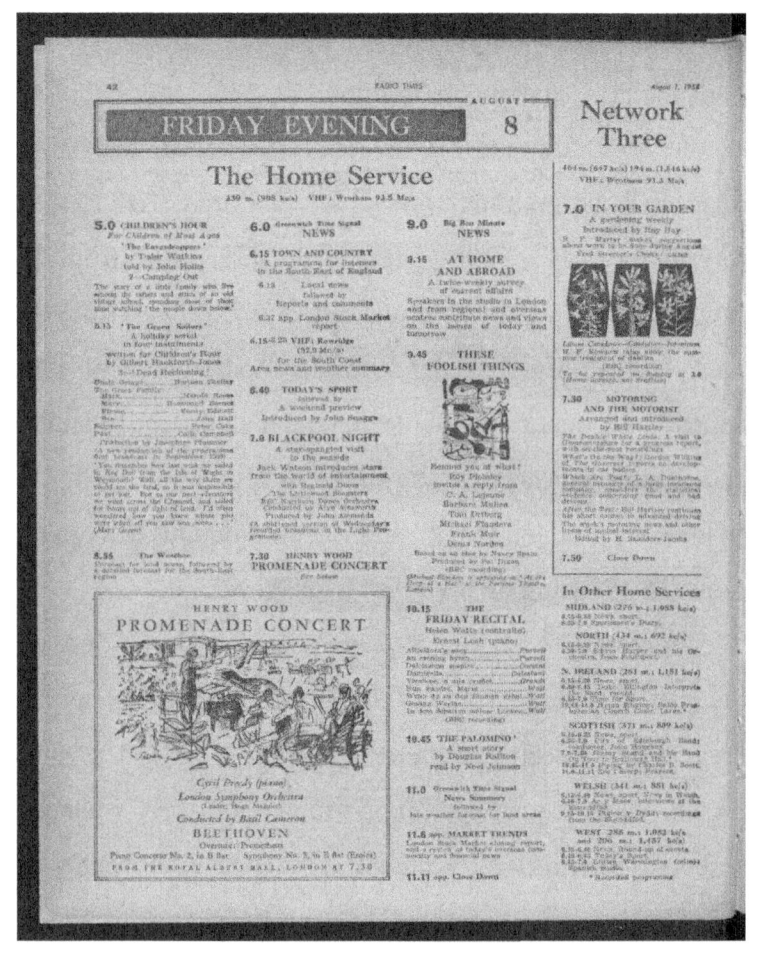

These Foolish Things

Friday 4th July - and again on various other dates in 1958 - Flanders appeared on Roy Plomley's[205] show *These*

Foolish Things (based upon an idea by Nancy Spain - remember her?) on the Home Service at 9.45 p.m. I wonder what he made of another participant, Tom Dreiberg.[206] We do not know what *his* contribution represented.

There was a topical diversion on television on Wednesday 22nd October at 4.15 p.m. when on *Mainly for Women* - introduced by presenter John Lindsay - Flanders read a story.

Thursday 30th October, and again on 20th November, Flanders – among other dates – appeared on the Light Programme at 5.30 p.m. in *Roundabout*. This affectionately remembered programme offered news, views and interviews. Flanders contribution was that he set yet another competition: this great competitor had clearly developed prowess as a competition setter.[207] He was the presenter on at least one occasion when among others he introduced Harry Belafonte and Connie Francis.[208]

A month later, on Thursday 6th November at 6.29 p.m. on the Light Programme Flanders participated – believe it or not – in the *Weather and News Headlines* – in which he

---

[205] Broadcaster and playwright: famous for *Desert Island Discs*
[206] Brazen and compulsive homosexual
[207] https://genome.ch.bbc.co.uk/24e90ad4b22846b1a8e5ab8f8029cf89
[208] Remember *Who's Sorry Now*?

set yet another competition. One wonders what it was and who won. *The Radio Times* announced that he was on the piano: which this writer very much questions.

At that time Alan Melville (referred to earlier) was a very popular broadcaster and television show host; indeed, he was one of Britain's first television stars. His programme *Alan Melville from A to Z* ran for two years from 1957. Among his four hundred guests were Flanders and Swann on 24th December at 7.30 p.m.[209] (in this case A-Z: F) What a cheerful start to Christmas!

Two days later on Friday 26th, the BBC broadcast the *Question-Masters' Brains Trust* on the Home Service at 11.15 a.m. Norman Fisher[210] then the present Question-Master together with some of the previous Question-Masters: Bernard Braden, Michael Flanders and Alan Melville answered questions set by regular members of the *Brains Trust*. Alan Bullock[211] was in the chair.

Yet again two days later, Sunday 28th December Flanders made the first of quite a number of appearances

---

[209] https://genome.ch.bbc.co.uk/schedules/service_bbc_television_service/1958-12-24

[210] Chief Education Office: City of Manchester

[211] A prolific and public-spirited historian, he founded an Oxford college and defined the nature of tyranny and evil in the 20th century: he was also an expert on bovine matters

over the years on *This Week's Good Cause*: this was broadcast on the Home Service at 10.25 a.m. On this occasion, he was appealing on behalf of the *Woodlarks Workshop Trust*.[212] This charity helps women who are so crippled that they cannot walk. They are able to use their hands and are given training and employment in toymaking: and are provided with a permanent happy home.

1959

Sunday 18th January at 7.00 p.m. Flanders and Swann, together with members of the London Bach Society and the boys of Hampstead Parish Church, introduced on television a programme of sacred music, with a popular flavour under the strapline *Meeting Point: Make a Joyful Noise unto God.*[213] It was broadcast from The Priory Church of St Bartholomew the Great in Smithfield.

Tuesday 26th May Flanders and Swann appeared at 9.20 p.m. on the Third Programme in *Not a Drum was Heard: The War Memoirs of General Gland* by Henry Reed. In this Flanders played a BBC Interviewer and a

---

[212] Still based in Farnham

[213] https://genome.ch.bbc.co.uk/a558586f2a6d4820b0e504bb76a16e1e

Russian interrogator. The general was a soldier-scholar who was obsessed by the sound of bells and wrote poetry in his spare time. The programme was repeated four times over the years.

Two years after Flanders and Swann's first recording - on 2nd May[214] - with the pair at the height of their fame, Martin returned to the Fortune Theatre to make the better-known 1959 stereo recording[215] - with exactly the same songs, but quite differently presented. Flanders talks more, the *Hippopotamus* song[216] has its second chorus in Russian and the interior designer can still remember why he hung a Northumbrian spoke-shaver's coracle on the wall. Sir George later talked about the problems of making the recording in the absence of voice microphones and said he was not sure whether it was. in fact, a better recording.[217]

Two years of singing also seemed to have done a great deal for the health of Flanders' remaining lung;[218] several

---

[214] Released 1960
[215] https://www.discogs.com/release/11359021-Michael-Flanders-And-Donald-Swann-At-The-Drop-Of-A-Hat
[216] Everybody sang it; they sang it in Russian, in Tongan and Indonesian. Audiences thought nothing of sitting in theatres and singing about mud and hippos, however surreal it might have felt later
[217] https://www.bbc.co.uk/sounds/play/b00d1025
[218] Amis, John: sleeve notes for *The Complete Flanders and Swann* CD set

notes (particularly the last 'mud') are held for considerably longer. The 1959 recording, which was made during their final performance at the Fortune Theatre, was more polished and in stereo. Sadly, it has become the definitive version.[219]

Swann recalls that he and Flanders had a lot of very grand (or at least famous!) people visit them back stage: but that he and Flanders never kept alcohol and did not entertain in their Dressing Room. Swann went home by bus and he would eat a poached egg in a nearby café.[220]

So, their run at the Fortune Theatre ended and Swann recalls that the heretofore mentioned Messrs Minster and Clift were very upset[221] because their golden goose was disappearing at the drop of a hat; as it were. They had made a fortune from the show.

The two artistes took three months off and then played at the Royal Lyceum Theatre, Edinburgh under the title *At the Drop of a Kilt* as part of the Edinburgh International Festival.[222] They commenced on 23rd August: the programme made it clear that 'every night tends to be

---

[219] https://thegawain.wordpress.com/2013/03/11/flanders-and-swann/
[220] Swann, Donald: Op. cit. p. 134
[221] Op. cit. p. 139
[222] An annual arts festival in Scotland, spread over the final three weeks in August

different.'[223] It was in this theatre that they played to over one thousand people for the very first time; it must have given them a charge. Swann recalls that Flanders developed a technique of playing to the front row: the rest of the audience behind them followed (a spontaneous backward movement)![224] The show then transferred to Broadway under its original title.[225]

---

[223] https://soundcloud.com/nfsaaustralia/flanders-and-swann-interviewed
[224] Op. cit. p. 140
[225] https://www.filmedlivemusicals.com/drop-another-hat.html

Second LP: recorded 2nd May 1959

1959 Edinburgh Festival programme

AT THE DOFF OF A HAT

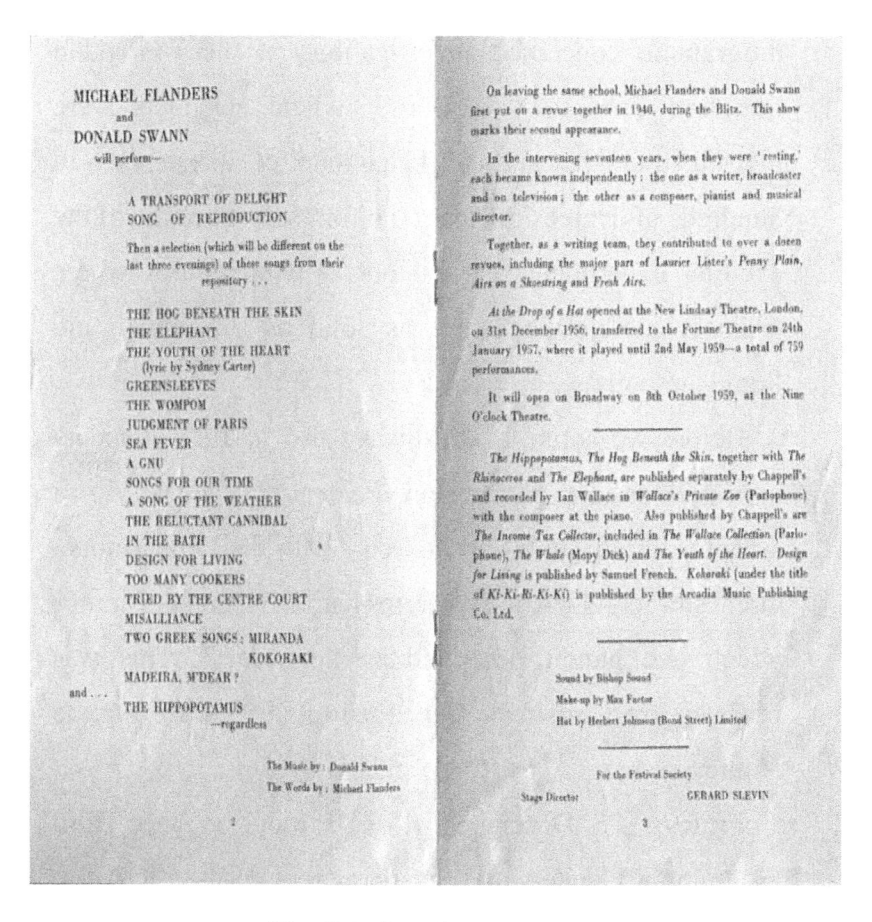

MICHAEL FLANDERS
and
DONALD SWANN
will perform—

A TRANSPORT OF DELIGHT
SONG OF REPRODUCTION

Then a selection (which will be different on the last three evenings) of these songs from their repository...

THE HOG BENEATH THE SKIN
THE ELEPHANT
THE YOUTH OF THE HEART
   (lyric by Sydney Carter)
GREENSLEEVES
THE WOMPOM
JUDGMENT OF PARIS
SEA FEVER
A GNU
SONGS FOR OUR TIME
A SONG OF THE WEATHER
THE RELUCTANT CANNIBAL
IN THE BATH
DESIGN FOR LIVING
TOO MANY COOKERS
TRIED BY THE CENTRE COURT
MISALLIANCE
TWO GREEK SONGS: MIRANDA
                 KOKORAKI
MADEIRA, M'DEAR?
and...
THE HIPPOPOTAMUS
   —regardless

The Music by: Donald Swann
The Words by: Michael Flanders

On leaving the same school, Michael Flanders and Donald Swann first put on a revue together in 1948, during the Blitz. This show marks their second appearance.

In the intervening seventeen years, when they were 'resting,' each became known independently; the one as a writer, broadcaster and on television; the other as a composer, pianist and musical director.

Together, as a writing team, they contributed to over a dozen revues, including the major part of Laurier Lister's *Penny Plain*, *Airs on a Shoestring* and *Fresh Airs*.

At the Drop of a Hat opened at the New Lindsay Theatre, London, on 31st December 1956, transferred to the Fortune Theatre on 24th January 1957, where it played until 2nd May 1959—a total of 759 performances.

It will open on Broadway on 8th October 1959, at the Nine O'clock Theatre.

The Hippopotamus, *The Hog Beneath the Skin*, together with *The Rhinoceros* and *The Elephant*, are published separately by Chappell's and recorded by Ian Wallace in *Wallace's Private Zoo* (Parlophone) with the composer at the piano. Also published by Chappell's are *The Income Tax Collector*, included in *The Wallace Collection* (Parlophone), *The Whale* (Mopy Dick) and *The Youth of the Heart*. *Design for Living* is published by Samuel French. *Kokoraki* (under the title of *Ki-Ki-Ri-Ki-Ki*) is published by the Arcadia Music Publishing Co. Ltd.

Sound by Bishop Sound
Make-up by Max Factor
Hat by Herbert Johnson (Bond Street) Limited

For the Festival Society
Stage Director   GERARD SLEVIN

The Edinburgh programme
- note its flexibility and its
advance notice of the opening on Broadway

10th September[226] Flanders provided the commentary in *Cold* at 8.45 a.m. on television. This strange sounding programme concerned investigations at the Clarendon Research Laboratory, Oxford[227] where scientists were investigating the strange behaviour of substances in hundreds of degrees of frost. The film showed some of the exciting experiments carried out at temperatures where ordinary mercury becomes as solid as a hammer and liquid air 'boils'.

Before we come to Broadway, also in 1959 Flanders appeared as the narrator in *Peter and the Wolf* - a symphonic fairy tale for children - with the Philharmonia Orchestra conducted by Efrem Kurtz:[228] an appearance which one pundit described as 'legendary'. This was repeated on Christmas Day 1961 at 5.25 p.m. on the Home Service.

Friday 11th December at 9.20 p.m. on the Third programme Flanders and Swann again appeared in *Not a Drum was Heard*.

By now in the United States, Christmas 1959 Flanders had a top-twenty hit with the Michael Sammes Singers with their Parlophone recording of *A Little Drummer Boy*

---

[226] Re-broadcast on 27th October

[227] The Laboratory, located on Parks Road within the Science Area in Oxford University, is part of the Department of Physics

[228] A British orchestra based at the Royal Festival Hall founded in 1945 by Walter Legge; a classical music record producer for EMI

which was issued as a single disc:[229] and as part of a compilation EP issued at the same time (with introductions by Flanders) *The Christmas Story*. [230]

Parlophone 1959 EP

---

[229] *With The Youth of the Heart* on the flip side: made #20 in the Top 20
[230] First recorded in 1951 by the Trapp Family, the song was further popularized by a 1958 recording by the Harry Simeone Chorale

CHAPTER FOUR
ACROSS THE POND

In October 1959 Flanders and Swann took their show to New York: it was perceived as a very small very British revue.[231] The producer was Alexander H. Cohen. He was 'one of the last great eccentrics on Broadway;'[232] a groundbreaking American impresario *and* a great Anglophile.[233] He will always be remembered with appreciation as the man who brought Flanders and Swann to Broadway under the auspices of the Nine O'clock

---

[231] https://books.google.co.uk/books?id=oWLRDwAAQBAJ&pg=PA11&lpg=PA11&dq=at+the+drop+of+a+hat+flanders+and+swann&source=bl&ots=yYJsA3QnAM&sig=ACfU3U1HI3c5Dhk_k7Gi61pH72iUEGduVw&hl=en&sa=X&ved=2ahUKEwjS3q7Lv5r9AhX7REEAHbrmCCU4RhDoAXoECAQQAw#v=onepage&q=at%20the%20drop%20of%20a%20hat%20flanders%20and%20swann&f=false

[232] https://books.google.co.uk/books?id=Z9ECAAAAMBAJ&pg=PA40&lpg=PA40&dq=shubert+theatre+flanders+and+swann&source=bl&ots=z6qi8FduNN&sig=ACfU3U30TkF4wgsdJTA-nC5t6NjtlnqxIQ&hl=en&sa=X&ved=2ahUKEwjP-qvTjdb7AhVLe8AKHdwTBUk4ChDoAXoECAUQAw#v=onepage&q=shubert%20theatre%20flanders%20and%20swann&f=false

[233] Amis, John: *Dropping the Hat Again*, Radio 2 documentary, 12th January 1997

Theatre; even though he did not break even until they went on a national tour[234] (a surprising statistic seeing that the only prop was a piano and a hat stand!).

After seeing the show in London in May 1957, Cohen wrote to Flanders and Swann "I am sure you will be happy and interested to know that we were all in accord that your presentation has universal appeal and would easily be accepted here as successfully as in the West End. Only minor alterations are necessary." In June, Cohen placed an advertisement in *The New York Times* announcing that Flanders and Swann were to appear in the States under his management. It seems that the duo were most unhappy about this advert. In a letter dated 5th September, Cohen expressed his deep regret at the "premature announcement" and apologized profusely "for any embarrassment that it may have caused you… The incident is most regrettable." Contracts were finally signed in June 1958.[235] Flanders was the first actor in a wheelchair to perform on Broadway: one critic made the imbecilic comment that at some point Flanders "could surely step out of his chair."[236] Swann wrote that it was a

---

[234] Swann, Donald. Op. cit. p. 163
[235] https://www.filmedlivemusicals.com/at-the-drop-hat.html
[236] https://www.filmedlivemusicals.com/blog/up-close-with-flanders-swann

theatrical and verbal experiment as the whole show had to be re-thought through with a different audience in mind.[237]

The *New Yorker* reported that they arrived on 18th September, the day the Manufacturers Bank was robbed. Crowds had gathered and all the traffic had been held up. "Oh yes, this is what we expected," they are reported as joking.[238]

At the Drop of a Hat opened to rave reviews on 8th October at the eight hundred seat John Golden Theatre. John Golden leased the theatre in 1936 and renamed it after himself;[239] as one does. Americans fell about at the Britishness of the show.[240] Time magazine wrote 'The humour of Flanders' and Swann's revue resembles a martini: it goes down smoothly, is slightly sly and definitely dry.'[241] One critic wrote 'They sent the wrong chaps over in 1775; if George III had sent these boys over, they might not have lost a colony.'[242] In the *New York Herald Tribune,* Walter Kerr wrote, 'Whatever it is that

---

[237] Swann, Donald. Op. cit. p. 159
[238] https://www.newyorker.com/magazine/1959/12/12/flanders-and-swann
[239] https://en.wikipedia.org/wiki/John_Golden_Theatre
[240] Amiss, John: BBC documentary, 27th December 1994
[241] http://content.time.com/time/subscriber/article/0,33009,836861-2,00.html
[242] Swann, Donald. Op. cit. p. 164

runs through both these gentlemen's veins it makes them lively, witty, literate, ingratiating, explosively funny and excellent company for a daffy[243] and delightful evening.'[244] To find a niche for this type of show was surely unique:[245] but, of course, Flanders and Swann were unique.

Cohen was a flamboyant live wire and turned the opening night into a big English event. He blanketed the façade of the Golden with posters of then current London hits. He offered tea and biscuits in the theatre: and served fish and chips to punters as they left at 11.00 p.m. You could hear Big Ben chiming: there was a man dressed up as a British Bobby patrolling the premises. Free sherry was offered in the bars. They sold the Daily Express and Daily Mail outside the theatre. He flew over *The Happy Wanderers*;[246] a bunch of Leicester Square buskers.[247] His

---

[243] Silly / mildly eccentric
[244] *At the Drop of a Hat in New York*, The Times, 10th October 1959, p. 9
[245] https://books.google.co.uk/books?id=oWLRDwAAQBAJ&pg=PA11&lpg=PA11&dq=at+the+drop+of+a+hat+flanders+and+swann&source=bl&ots=yYJsA3QnAM&sig=ACfU3U1HI3c5Dhk_k7Gi61pH72iUEGduVw&hl=en&sa=X&ved=2ahUKEwjS3q7Lv5r9AhX7REEAHbrmCCU4RhDoAXoECAQQAw#v=onepage&q=at%20the%20drop%20of%20a%20hat%20flanders%20and%20swann&f=false
[246] https://twitter.com/bbcarchive/status/1366710123146584066?lang=en-GB
[247] Swann, Donald. Op. cit, p. 162

tour de force was to create a fog on 44th Street[248] which was so lifelike and effective that the police asked Cohen to move it along.[249] This must be the only recorded example of fog effectively being moved on. No wonder Cohen failed to make a profit on Broadway. The production closed on the 14th May 1960 after 216 performances.

During the period 1957 through 1962 the *Jack Paar Show* on NBC was a pre-eminent chat show broadcast late at night. At first, the show was called *Tonight Starring Jack Paar*; after 1959 it was officially known as *The Jack Paar Show*. Parr was often unpredictable and emotional: he might of course have been tired and emotional. Swann wrote that it was very important to be on *Jack Paar* (and *Ed Sullivan* more so) and, he said, you might not want to do so.[250] Flanders and Swann appeared on the show twice on 19th October 1959 and 14th January 1960.[251]

---

[248] Amiss, John: *Dropping the Hat Again*, Radio 2 documentary, 12th January 1997
[248] Op. cit.
[249] Swann, Donald: Op. cit. p. 162
[250] Swann, Donald. Op. cit. p. 172
[251] https://ctva.biz/US/TalkShow/TonightShow_1959-60_JackPaar_s3.htm

During the touring period the pair were commissioned - and this was very unusual, it was one of few they ever accepted - to write a song for the *American Bookseller's Association*. The result is *Vendor Librorum Floreat* – a pleasing song to the tune of "Widecombe Fair."[252/253] It was recorded at Gotham Production Studios on 27th April 1960 and issued as a one-sided single by the *New York Times*.[254] Fans who play the CD collection in disc order from the *Hat Trick - Flanders and Swann Collector's Edition* will encounter this song last of all; the final piece of their music released on CD.[255]

---

[252] https://www.youtube.com/watch?v=RW2GYfOMa20

[253] https://rateyourmusic.com/release/single/flanders_and_swann/vendor_librorum_floreat/

[254] https://www.youtube.com/watch?v=RW2GYfOMa20

[255] https://thegawain.wordpress.com/2013/03/11/flanders-and-swann/

The John Golden Theatre

New York Times one-sided single

*Flyer for New York's
latest sensation*

Programme for the first US production

*Another flyer
as they went from strength to strength*

AT THE DOFF OF A HAT

Yet another promo!

AT THE DOFF OF A HAT

NOTICE: — The exit indicated by a red light and sign, nearest to the seat you occupy, is the shortest route to the street.
In the event of emergency, please do not run — WALK TO THAT EXIT.
City Ordinance prohibits smoking in this theatre except in the outer lobby.

SEASON 1960-61

No. 3

Week Beg. Monday, Nov. 7 at 9 P.M.
Matinees Wednesday and Saturday at 2 P.M.

A Theater Guild Attraction
Alexander H. Cohen
presents
THE NINE O'CLOCK THEATRE PRODUCTION

MICHAEL FLANDERS and DONALD SWANN

in their After-dinner Farrago . . .

At the drop of a hat -

Produced in association with Joseph I. Levine
Lighting by Ralph Alswang

MICHAEL FLANDERS
and
DONALD SWANN
will perform
SONG OF REPRODUCTION
THE HOG BENEATH THE SKIN
A TRANSPORT OR DELIGHT
THE YOUTH OF THE HEART
(lyrics by Sydney Carter)

PLEASE DO NOT LIGHT MATCHES OR SMOKE IN THIS THEATRE. IT IS NOT ONLY DANGEROUS BUT IT IS A VIOLATION OF THE LAW AND ANY OFFENDER IS LIABLE TO ARREST.

— 3 —

Do not light matches at the Golden Theatre

On their arrival in the United States, Flanders had jokingly told the press that he was looking for an American bride:[256] as one does. Having opened on Broadway on 8th October, on 31st December Flanders married Claudia Davis[257] who he had met within twenty days of arriving in the States. Claudia was the daughter of journalist Claud Cockburn[258] and stepdaughter of Professor Robert Gorham Davis (whom Flanders had known in England).[259] Cockburn, born in China, was a Communist and was involved with *Private Eye* in its early days: he was a bit of a personality.

Claudia had been an American fan of *At the Drop of a Hat* and had helped with its promotion during the Previews before its Broadway opening.[260] She said that, at that time, Previews were a new thing and that she had dragooned her friends free of charge into attending to bulk out the audience.[261] So, he proposed less than three months after they met. Flanders said that he much enjoyed

---

[256] Swann, Donald. Op. cit. p. 159
[257] Aged 26
[258] A cousin of Evelyn Waugh
[259] Professor of English at Columbia University, New York City
[260] Amiss, John: *Dropping the Hat Again,* Radio 2 documentary, 12th January 1997
[260] Op. cit.
[261] Op. cit.

working in the US having met and married an American girl. 1st January 1960 the *New York Times* reported the happy event.[262]

One of life's very happy moments

---

[262] https://www.nytimes.com/1960/01/01/archives/michael-flanders-weds-costar-of-revue-and-miss-claudia-c-davis.html?auth=login-google1tap&login=google1tap

Flanders and his wife had two daughters, Laura (1961) and Stephanie (1968). After their marriage, Claudia and her husband toured the world with Flanders' and Swann's shows. She was technical manager and creative consultant. "I only produce the show; Claudia has the hard job - producing me," Flanders was often quoted as saying.[263]

---

[263] https://www.independent.co.uk/arts-entertainment/obituary-claudia-flanders-1173922.html

CHAPTER FIVE
1960 - THE THEATRE GUILD TOUR

Back in the motherland, Thursday 26th May at 10.00 p.m. on the Third Programme and again on Tuesday 21st June, Flanders appeared in *Voices in the Air*: a programme of words and music from all over Britain. All we know is that Flanders provided words!

Saturday 8th October Flanders appeared on Network Three[264] at 10.15 a.m. as the narrator in *Stereophony*. Once again, the programme included a record of Prokofiev's *Peter and the Wolf* played by the Philharmonia Orchestra conducted by Efrem Kurtz (to which we referred earlier). This was a demonstration of stereophonic sound which was a new innovation (and a great novelty) at the time.

Then off to the States once more. Swann wrote that by this point Flanders had reached a very high point with his theatrical skills: 'He was at his very peak.'[265] It is worth

---

[264] Network Three replaced the Third Programme. It began broadcasting on 30th September 1957 and ended on 29th September 1967

reflecting that Swann wrote this of a man whose ambition had been to go into the theatre and who had only made it through the back door so to speak: and, to boot, in a wheelchair. Some achievement. Flanders acquired a more sensible automobile (into which he could get his wheelchair) (it was undoubtedly a large American limo) and they mostly drove across the states from city to city.

At the Drop of a Hat toured widely latter 1960 through early 1961; visiting many cities in the US;[266] plus Toronto:

October 25th McCarter Theatre 8.30 p.m. Princeton, NJ
(a university audience, of course)[267]
Wilmington, NC
Pittsburgh, PA
Cincinnati, OH
Des Moines, IO
Denver, CO

---

[265] Swann, Donald. Op. cit. p. 167
[266] https://www.filmedlivemusicals.com/drop-another-hat.html
[267] https://books.google.co.uk/books?id=8hJbAAAAYAAJ&pg=RA4-PA3&lpg=RA4-PA3&dq=Princeton+%2B+Flanders+and+Swann&source=bl&ots=_TulWRKeAO&sig=ACfU3U0DpCD1IHT3PdkJVOwBEaCOPmS_7Q&hl=en&sa=X&ved=2ahUKEwjQlKvf4L_7AhWPY8AKHVQuARwQ6AF6BAgkEAM#v=onepage&q=Princeton%20%2B%20Flanders%20and%20Swann&f=false

7th – 12th New Haven, CN

Los Angeles, CA

San Francisco, CA

January 1961 The Auditorium Theatre, Saint Paul, MN[268]

16th – 21st January 1961 American Theatre, St Louis, MO

5th February Blackstone Theatre, Chicago, IL[269]

13th – 25th February, Shubert Theatre, Detroit, MI

27th February – March 11th Toronto, Canada[270]

Swann described it as a wonderful cumulative experience. Flanders would enter a new city: he would suss out what was going and what its idiosyncrasies were: and then add two or three wonderful lines to the show to make a hit with the local press. The two of them appeared for a fortnight in the larger cities and for a week in the smaller ones. Swann remarked how strange it was appearing in a Midwest city like Des Moines (where they did a one-night stand).

Someone uncomprehending in Cincinnati had asked for their money back! When reimbursed but also moved

---

[268] Demolished 1982
[269] Now the Merle Reskin Theatre
[270] https://web.archive.org/web/20141129213114/http://www.nyanko.pwp.blueyonder.co.uk/fas/hatshow.html

to the front stall he yelled that he could not understand a word of it (mind you, Swann *was* singing in Russian!). Swann says that it was a tour de force on Flanders part to persuade Midwestern audiences that London literary humour was funny: but he did it.[271]

So, the American show featured Flanders and Swann and their single piano. As usual there were no props. As the *New York Herald Tribune* so wonderfully put it, just two men 'completely surrounded by talent'.[272] Another notice described them affectionately as 'two men and a lamp.'[273]

It was, as Flanders announced as he introduced the evening, "A revue without scenery, without costume - except for our normal evening wear, worn throughout the Empire - and also without a cast." Yet Flanders and Swann filled the stage with their larger-than-life characters and creatures and conquered their audience with their charmingly irreverent and idiosyncratic humour.[274] If they

---

[271] Swann, Donald. Op. cit. p. 170
[272] https://www.comedy.co.uk/features/comedy_chronicles/remarkable-legacy-of-flanders-and-swann/
[273] Op. cit. p. 161
[274] http://briansibleysblog.blogspot.com/2008/02/who-says-nostalgia-isnt-what-it-was.html

did it today some blithering idiot would complain about something.

American Theatre St Louis, programme

They appeared 16th – 21st January at the St Louis American Theatre.[275] This was followed later by appearances at the Shubert Theatre, Detroit from 13th to 25th February. The Shubert was located on the southeast corner of Shelby and Lafayette streets and was last operated as the Shubert-Lafayette. It was demolished in the summer of 1964. Today the site is a parking garage.[276]

---

[275] Originally named The Orpheum, this landmark was located at 416 North Ninth Street. It was later renamed the Roberts Orpheum Theater and was then sold and closed

[276] https://historicdetroit.org/buildings/shubert-lafayette-theatre

American Theatre, St Louis

Chicago!

programme

ON STAGE
THE MAGAZINE FOR THE SHUBERT THEATRE

♦ ADVERTISING
♦ PUBLISHING
♦ PUBLICITY

published by the
RUSHELLE AGENCY, INC.
ALSO PUBLISHERS OF GUEST AND SKYLINER MAGAZINES
S. Richard Uday, Editor & Publisher

WO. 2-0606
505 PARK AVE. BLDG.

VOL. 10 — MONDAY, FEB. 13 THROUGH SATURDAY, FEB. 25, 1961 — NO. 14

Alexander H. Cohen
presents
The Nine O'Clock Theatre Production
of
MICHAEL FLANDERS and DONALD SWANN
in their After-dinner Farrago . . .

At The Drop of A Hat

Produced in association with Joseph I. Levine

MICHAEL FLANDERS
and
DONALD SWANN
will perform —
SONG OF REPRODUCTION
THE HOG BENEATH THE SKIN
A TRANSPORT OF DELIGHT
THE YOUTH OF THE HEART
(lyrics by Sydney Carter)
GREENSLEEVES
THE WOMPOM
SEA FEVER
A GNU
JUDGMENT OF PARIS
SONGS FOR OUR TIME
Interval of twelve minutes

DETROIT'S FINEST IN
- FOOD
- SPORTS
- ENTERTAINMENT
- CATERING

THEATRE PARTY NIGHTS —
Ticket - Dinner - Transportation

JIM CORNELIUS'
Knife & Fork Club
FIRST & HOWARD WO 2-8981

ON STAGE • Page 3

Detroit programme

Flanders and Swann
at the much lamented O'Keefe Centre

Programme - O'Keefe Centre

Swann remembered Toronto with great affection. The O'Keefe Centre (the most handsome theatre that he ever played) was on the North American touring circuit and was the largest in Canada. It later became the Hummingbird Centre for the Performing Arts: and then later still morphed into the Sony Centre. Alas, it is now the Meridian Hall.

Carling O'Keefe[277] was a Canadian brewing company. Flanders began the performance by saying "See what you can do if you return the empties."[278] The audience fell about. Swann recalled that Toronto theatre critics asked 'why is this audience of 3,000 enjoying themselves so much.' Flanders thought that their stay there was the best that they achieved.[279]

The American tour was the biggest **low-key event** that many could remember; no one wanted it to end. Flanders' friend the critic Michael Meyer noted that "The combination of Flanders' genial yet caustic lyrics and Swann's tuneful music, together with the contrast between Flanders' robust exuberance and the prim appearance of Swann, exerted a seemingly *universal* appeal."

In what was a master stroke of originality, the Home Service broadcast a programme at 8.15 p.m. on 29th August 1961; *At the Drop of a Stetson*. Their chum

---

[277] Later *Canadian Breweries*
[278] Swann, Donald. Op. cit. p. 174
[279] Op. cit. p. 176

Sydney Carter[280] talked to Flanders and Swann. This was followed at 8.45 p.m. by excerpts from *At the Drop of a Hat*.

Some people considered that Flanders' lyrics were the wittiest and best crafted that the musical stage had heard since those of W. S. Gilbert.[281] Certainly, Gascoigne believed that Flanders' lyrics, at their best, approached the intricate ease of Gilbert.[282] Praise indeed. Although the New York Times obituary writer (perhaps) had some reservations in saying 'Flanders' lyrics faintly resembled some of the funnier ones of Sir William S. Gilbert, poking fun at British middleclass attitudes and customs. In performing them, Flanders pretended not to notice that some of his rhymes were horribly laboured - which made them all the funnier - or that his outrageous puns made the strongest men cringe.'[283] So, there you have it.

---

[280] A songsmith: he wrote the words of a song recorded live by Flanders and Swann at the Blackstone Theatre, Chicago in February 1961

[281] English dramatist, librettist, poet and illustrator: best known for his collaboration with composer Arthur Sullivan

[282] Gascoigne, Bamber: *Theatre*, The Observer, 6th October 1963, p. 26

[283] https://www.nytimes.com/1975/04/16/archives/michael-flanders-is-dead-at-53-humoriststar-of-drop-of-a-hat.html

Incidentally, and regarding those lyrics, Swann opined that the greatest response to them was from children![284] Further, he commented on Flanders' strong verbal sense of punning and an ability to comment humorously on the things that he could see around him.[285]

---

[284] Swann, Donald. Op. cit. p. 51
[285] Op. cit. p. 105

CHAPTER SIX
1961 - INTERREGNUM

Having not set fire to the theatre in New York, on a visit to Switzerland in 1961 the duo played the Théâtre de la cour St-Pierre, Geneva,[286] Friday 12th May at Theatre de Vevey and then Lausanne.[287]

On Wednesday 10th May, Flanders and Swann appeared on *Sweet Corn* on the Light Programme at 8.31 p.m. Whatever it was, this featured music for modern squares, with Bill Shepherd directing the Sweet Corn Orchestra and Chorus. Whatever you might call Flanders and Swann, this writer does not believe that either would be categorized as a 'square' (incidentally that is an almost forgotten term: as well as it being a long-forgotten programme!)

Flanders also appeared as the narrator in the documentary *Falling in Love*.[288] It was produced by ATV

---

[286] 16th May: Berger, Leon: *Hat-Tricks: guide to the songs*
[287] https://web.archive.org/web/20141129213114/http://www.nyanko.pwp.blueyonder.co.uk/fas/hatshow.html

and broadcast on 31st May: by now he knew something about the subject.

Later, on Friday 23rd June, Flanders appeared as the author in *Mr Biedermann and the Fire-Raisers* at 8.30 p.m. on the Third Programme. This was a play for broadcasting translated by Michael Bullock in which a witty Swiss author introduced listeners to a self-satisfied small-town citizen whose conduct as an employer and a manufacturer of hair restoratives may not have been above reproach but who had a sentimental streak. It sounds like the kind of play that would have gone down well in West Hatch.

Flanders and Swann continued to make numerous BBC radio appearances; one of which was *Monday Night at Home* – a selection of recorded wit, music, and humour – on Friday 26th June at 7.30 p.m.

Tuesday 18th July the pair appeared in *Four of a Kind* on the Home Service at 9.10 a.m. This was an eccentric programme featuring four participants making contributions about bus travel: for example, Arthur Tarnowski[289] told listeners how to get to India by bus for an outlay of only £34.

---

[288] https://www.imdb.com/title/tt3756964/?ref_=ttfc_fc_tt
[289] Polish aristocrat: also paralyzed from polio but one who who still wrote travel books

Flanders appeared on *Review* on the Home Service on Monday 7th August at 5.15 p.m. – one of many appearances on the programme. He introduced a monthly reflection on current films, plays and art exhibitions; as well as the people concerned with them. On one other appearance W. A. Darlington (the doyen of theatre critics) made an appearance. Flanders also appeared on *At the Drop of a Needle* (in which he played records for listeners' enjoyment.[290]

In addition, there was *Round Britain Quiz* on which he appeared on Thursday 28th September on the Home Service at 1.10 p.m. - and on other dates later on - and on which he was Quizmaster. This programme – broadcast since 1947 – is the oldest quiz still broadcast on the BBC. Teams from various regions of the UK go head-to-head: each being given four multi-part cryptic questions.[291] Lateral thought is required! Evidentially Flanders clearly had a gift for mastering quizzes.

On Friday 6th October, Flanders fronted BBC television's *Let's Imagine* for the first time. This was an

---

290

https://genome.ch.bbc.co.uk/search/0/20?q=Michael+Flanders&after=1961-01-01T00%3A00%3A00.000Z&before=1961-12-31T23%3A59%3A59.999Z#top

[291] Ones with hidden meanings

inventive programme that ran into two series. Flanders appeared in editions 2 and 3 of Series Two. (One example was, *Let's Imagine – Living in a Haunted House*.[292] He enquired into stories of ghosts; told by people who had studied the supernatural or had suffered ghosts thrust upon them.

On Friday 20th October he appeared in *Let's Imagine – Behind the Front Doors* in which he looked inside some houses in a fashionable part of London inhabited by beautiful people. Among those *at home* in Montpelier Square[293] that day was Leslie Caron.[294/295]

Thursday 26th October at 5.31 p.m. on the Light Programme, Flanders introduced a daily round of music, news, views, and information on all manner of topics on *Roundabout*. Michael Holliday (famous for the *Runaway Train*) - who had a mental breakdown the same year - was one of the contributors: but we do not know if it was brought on by his appearance on this programme.

---

[292] https://genome.ch.bbc.co.uk/search/0/20?filt=c6795cefa3506c95ad3f5836787f51a0

[293] Residential garden square Knightsbridge

[294] French-American actress and dancer

[295] https://genome.ch.bbc.co.uk/schedules/service_bbc_television_service/1961-10-20

Flanders made further appearances on the programme and on one Frank Sinatra made a guest appearance; he was in London for a concert later at the Royal Festival Hall.

Tuesday 31st October[296] the BBC broadcast *Television and the World* at 9.25 p.m. with Flanders the perennial narrator. The programme interestingly journeyed through five continents seeking to provide an impression of the impact of television on peoples of different civilisations.[297] They might think of doing a follow up programme today focussed on the impact on the world of social media.

In November and December, the BBC featured Flanders and Swann's LP: *The Bestiary of Flanders and Swann* over two episodes on the Third Programme on 29th October at 7.30 p.m. and the 26th December. *The Radio Times* reported that 'the dictionary defines *bestiary* as *a mediaeval work describing the animal kingdom, real and fable, allegorised for edification'*. The BBC went on to say that the programme was designed for 'Third Programme listeners and their children'.[298]

Sunday 10th December Flanders made a second appearance on *This Week's Good Cause*: this time

---

[296] Repeated two months later
[297] https://genome.ch.bbc.co.uk/53ccc323f2b04e1fb417a8e1222b4de5
[298] https://genome.ch.bbc.co.uk/7172dec0c2de48578d2caab02ac24596

appealing on behalf of the *Royal Hospital and Home for Incurables*, Putney: now known as *The Royal Hospital for Neuro-disability*. This facility is an independent medical charity that provides rehabilitation and long-term care to people with complex neurological disabilities caused by damage to the brain or other parts of the nervous system.

Sunday 31st December Flanders spoke the commentary on the BBC programme *Television and the World*. The reviews[299] - stimulating and enthralling - were outstanding: as indeed they were of most of Richard Cawston's work.

1962

Friday 26th January saw Flanders appear as the storyteller in *Mossy Green Theatre* on the Home Service at 5.15 p.m. This was a serial play in five parts (adapted by Mary Dunn from her book; with music by Alan Paul). It related the story of when Waney built a theatre of moss and twigs in the New Forest and animals and birds organised a production of the pantomime Cinderella.

BBC television introduced a series called *Sunday Story* running from 1961-1968. It broadcast at 6.45 p.m. starting

---

[299] https://genome.ch.bbc.co.uk/8cc11f1145df470ca06cf6104a8991fd

on 25th March. Tom Fleming was a regular story teller but when the *Story of Peter* was broadcast Flanders became the narrator of all seven episodes: he related the story of Saint Peter.[300]

29th March was Press Night for the Royal Shakespeare Company's production of Brecht's *The Caucasian Chalk Circle* at the Aldwych Theatre. Flanders was appearing as Arkadi Tscheidse: a renowned singer who has been brought in to entertain the members of a dairy farm and a fruit farm as they gather together to celebrate the triumph of reason in their deliberations over which farm should be assigned dominion over a lush and fertile valley. Arkadi narrates the story of *The Chalk Circle* for the farmers; creating a play-within-a-play.[301] It all sounds rather complicated.

Tuesday 29th May, Flanders and Swann appeared at The Scala Theatre[302] London in a charity revue *Take to the Hills!* A group of debutantes were photographed[303] doing a twist routine. The event was staged by High Society for

---

[300] https://www.imdb.com/title/tt13848264/fullcredits/?ref_=tt_ql_cl
[301] https://www.litcharts.com/lit/the-caucasian-chalk-circle/characters/arkadi-tscheidse
[302] Demolished 1969 after a fire
[303] https://www.gettyimages.co.uk/detail/news-photo/group-of-debutantes-rehearsing-a-twist-dance-routine-for-news-photo/573376717

charity: you would not write in those terms today! Princess Margaret and Tony Armstrong-Jones were in attendance; but, of course, they were beautiful people.

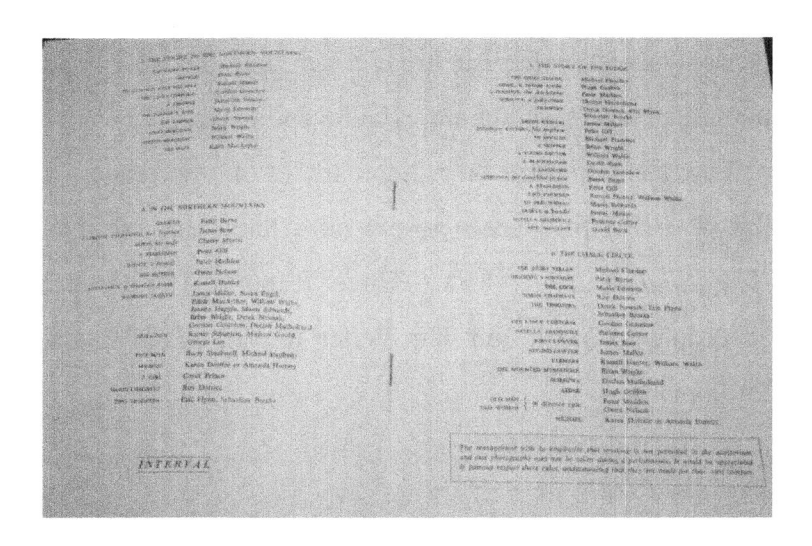

Excerpt from the Aldwych programme

Flanders appeared as the voice of Lorenzo in *Touches of Sweet Harmony* - music inspired by Shakespeare[304]/[305] It featured the Sinfonia of London[306] conducted by Robert Irving and Douglas Gamley. A recording was issued on a

---

[304] https://fampeople.com/cat-michael-flanders_4
[305] Issued on an LP: https://www.discogs.com/release/11610421-The-Sinfonia-Of-London-Conducted-By-Robert-Irving-2-And-Douglas-Gamley-Touches-Of-Sweet-Harmony-Musi
[306] An English session orchestra

His Master's Voice album. Once more, this time on Monday 30th July, Flanders was on the Light Programme at 2.15 p.m. presenting the first of a series of *Souvenir*: reminiscing with words and music from the past (which could amount to absolutely anything!). It was written by Derek Parker; a British broadcaster and the author of numerous works on literature, ballet and opera.

Flanders appeared on a Leomark LP as the reader of the whole of St Mark's gospel on a three-part set: *The New English Bible*.[307] Part Three featured The Gospel according to Mark and The Letter of Saint Paul to the Philippians.

---

[307] A new English translation published in 1961 by a bunch of lunatics: and best forgotten

HMV recording
Touches of Sweet Harmony

Taking into account the success of the 1959 album *At the Drop of a Hat*, it was later decided that the animal songs (minus the already well-known Gnu, Hippopotamus and Kokoraki) should be committed to a separate disc.

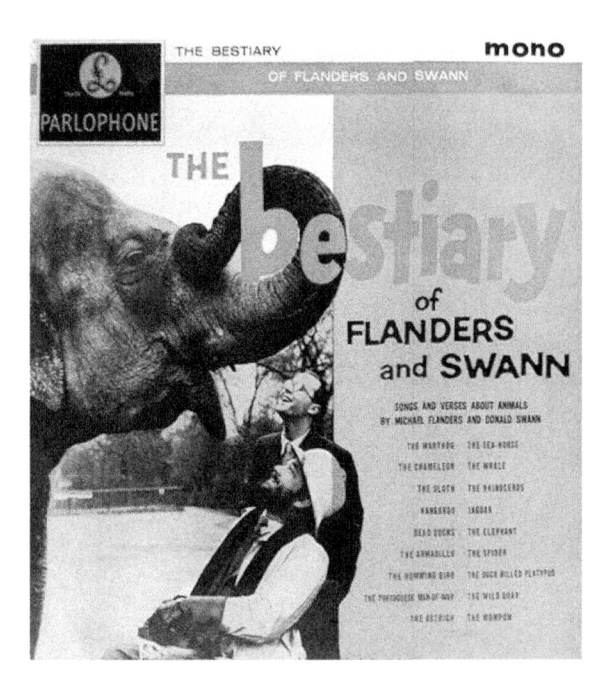

The Bestiary LP

This was to become the *Bestiary of Flanders and Swann*. It was produced with a studio recording and was released on Parlophone.[308] A few odds and ends about armadillos, ostriches and wompoms were included that had also been recorded in various parts of the world on an individual basis.[309] This recording was basically a collection of their animal songs originally made popular by Ian Wallace: an artiste that they much admired. Flanders often joked that they had several of his paintings in their collection. Wallace was an opera bass-baritone of distinction and often sang *The Gnu* and the ever popular *The Hippopotamus* (which has been translated into eighteen languages and whose chorus Swann was wont to sing in Russian).[310]

Tuesday 7th August at 8.40 p.m. saw Flanders back on television as a panel member in *It's My Opinion*. This was a television series which ran from 1958-65. In series Two, edition six (the only episode in which Flanders appeared) the good people of Gosport aired their views on a range of topics for spontaneous comment by Nemone Lethbridge, Lord Mancroft and Michael Flanders. It was chaired by the young David Dimbleby. I wonder why they chose the thinkers of Gosport.

---

[308] https://www.discogs.com/release/3025290-Michael-Flanders-And-Donald-Swann-The-Bestiary-Of-Flanders-And-Swann
[309] https://thegawain.wordpress.com/2013/03/11/flanders-and-swann/
[310] https://portal.newdaycards.com/johnlewis/login

On Friday 2nd November on the Home Service Flanders read *Cat up a Tree* - a short story - by novelist William Sansom.

Meanwhile, Flanders and Swann had resumed touring in the UK. They took in:

Canterbury

Oxford

Leeds

15th October Theatre Royal Newcastle-upon-Tyne

19th November Alexandra Theatre Birmingham

Aberdeen

Edinburgh

Liverpool

Manchester

Birmingham

Toronto, Canada[311]

---

[311]

https://web.archive.org/web/20141129213114/http://www.nyanko.pw p.blueyonder.co.uk/fas/hatshow.html

Birmingham: programme 1962

Saturday 10th November on the Third Programme at 6.30 p.m. Flanders participated in *How Not to Listen* which was repeated on Monday 31st December at 10.35 p.m. Along with Flanders, Stephen Potter and Joyce Grenfell (the latter two wrote the show) were contributing a new satirical revue to mark forty years of broadcasting. *How to Listen* having inaugurated the Third Programme in 1946.

CHAPTER SEVEN
1963

Tuesday 19th February also saw the transmission on television at 9.25 p.m. of *A Chance to Live*[312] directed by Michael Latham (responsible for some of the most influential factual programmes of his time).[313] This was a report on research work being done in Britain to help the disabled - including the Thalidomide victims - to live fuller lives by means of artificial aids. This masterpiece was narrated by Flanders; himself, of course, the chair-bound polio victim.

Flanders and Swann toured:

Richmond

Brighton

---

[312] https://genome.ch.bbc.co.uk/schedules/service_bbc_television_service/1963-02-19

[313] https://www.telegraph.co.uk/news/obituaries/1506899/Michael-Latham.html

4th – 9th February: Cambridge Arts Theatre

Coventry

Dublin, Eire

Oxford

Cambridge[314]

Coventry

Bristol

Guildford

---

[314] https://web.archive.org/web/20141129213114/http://www.nyanko.pwp.blueyonder.co.uk/fas/hatshow.html

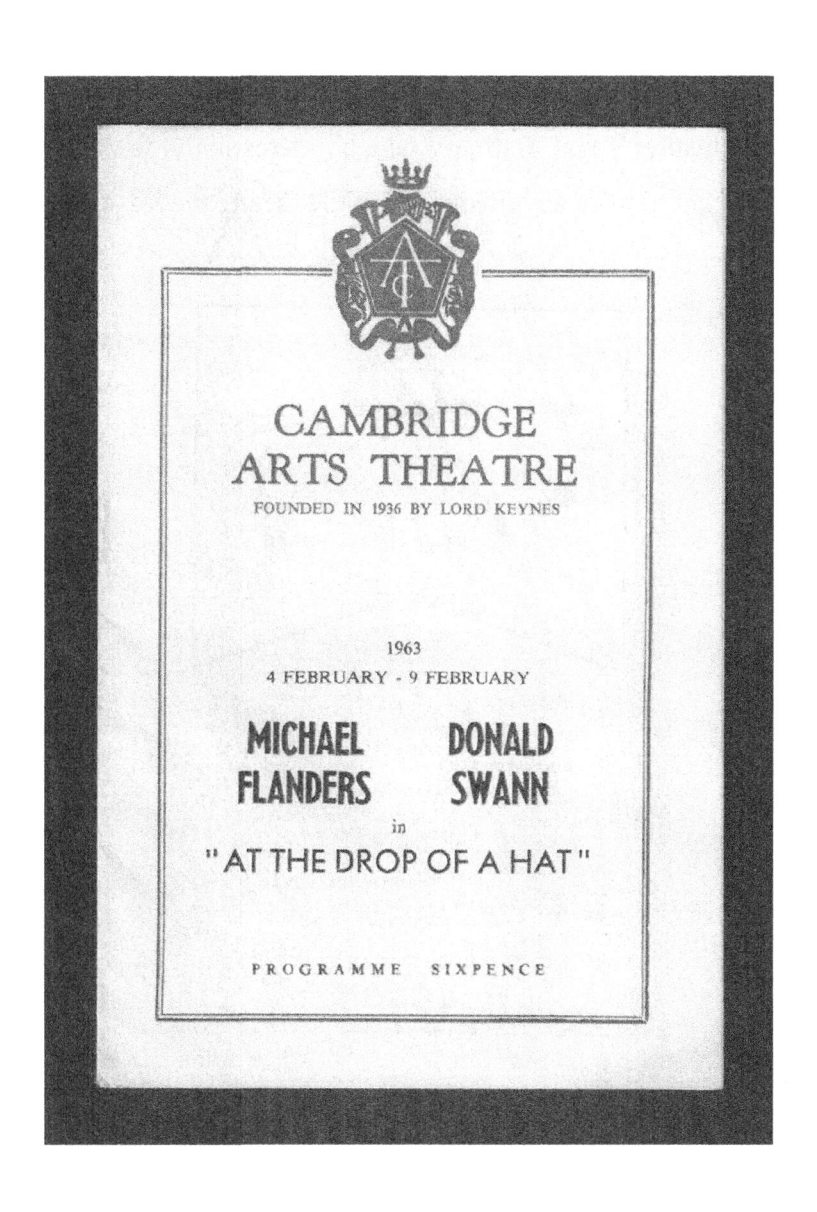

Cambridge Arts Theatre programme

~~~ and pre-London they did a warm up show at the Theatre Royal Bath of which interestingly few people seem to have any memory; but the theatre records do!

Theatre Royal Bath

September 1963

Flanders featured on another LP[315] in 1963; he spoke the voice of both Dromio of Syracuse *and* Dromio of Ephesus on *The Comedy of Error*s in the *Living Shakespeare* series: you sensed that he was a thespian to his fingertips.

On 17th August, Flanders and Swann appeared in *Take a Note* on television at 11.00 p.m. They took a look at some unusual reeds, bangers and whistles with the help of E. O. Pogson,[316] James McGilvery, Jeremy Montagu, Marylin Wailes, Cephas Howard and Alan Cooper. In another edition on Wednesday 20th November 1963 Flanders considered some musical oddities like serpents and heckelphones.[317]

Thursday 5th September at 9.45 a.m. on the Home Service Flanders was the narrator in *This Week's Composer* which featured Prokofiev's[318] *Peter and the Wolf:* a work and a composer of which he had rich knowledge.

Later that month, Friday 27th September, Flanders and Swann appeared at 10.00 p.m. on the Third Programme in

---

[315] Which came with a 32-page booklet containing the text
[316] British jazz instrumentalist (alto saxophone, reeds, flute and the like): he worked with bandleader Jack Payne
[317] A double reed instrument invented in the early 1900s by German instrument maker Wilhelm Heckel
[318] Russian composer

a rebroadcast of *Not a Drum was Heard: The War Memoirs of General Gland.*

Flanders and Swann opened at the Theatre Royal Haymarket on Wednesday 2nd October in *At the Drop of Another Hat;* a production that proved to be as successful as its predecessor at the Fortune Theatre. Later, in an Australian interview for Melbourne's *The Age* while discussing changes between the two shows,[319] Swann quipped "When we opened our new show... we decided to refurbish. We put another word in the title...and a new cover on the lamp."[320]

Flanders noted that in the new show they performed a programme of songs that had not before been sung in England.[321] The production ran until 21st March 1964. One of the new songs that attracted a fair amount of attention was *All Gall* in which Flanders' lyrics poked fun at French President Charles de Gaulle:[322] and suggested that he thought of himself as already being as important to France as Joan of Arc.[323]/[324]

---

[319] *The Age* is a daily newspaper in Melbourne that has been published since 1854
[320] https://www.filmedlivemusicals.com/drop-another-hat.html
[321] https://soundcloud.com/nfsaaustralia/flanders-and-swann-interviewed
[322] Died 9th November 1970
[323] As a patron saint

Theatre Royal Haymarket

---

[324] https://www.pressreader.com/uk/scottish-daily-mail/20150424/283059822922957

THEATRE ROYAL
HAYMARKET

MICHAEL   DONALD
FLANDERS   SWANN

with more of their
own words and music

AT THE DROP
OF
ANOTHER
HAT

Programme

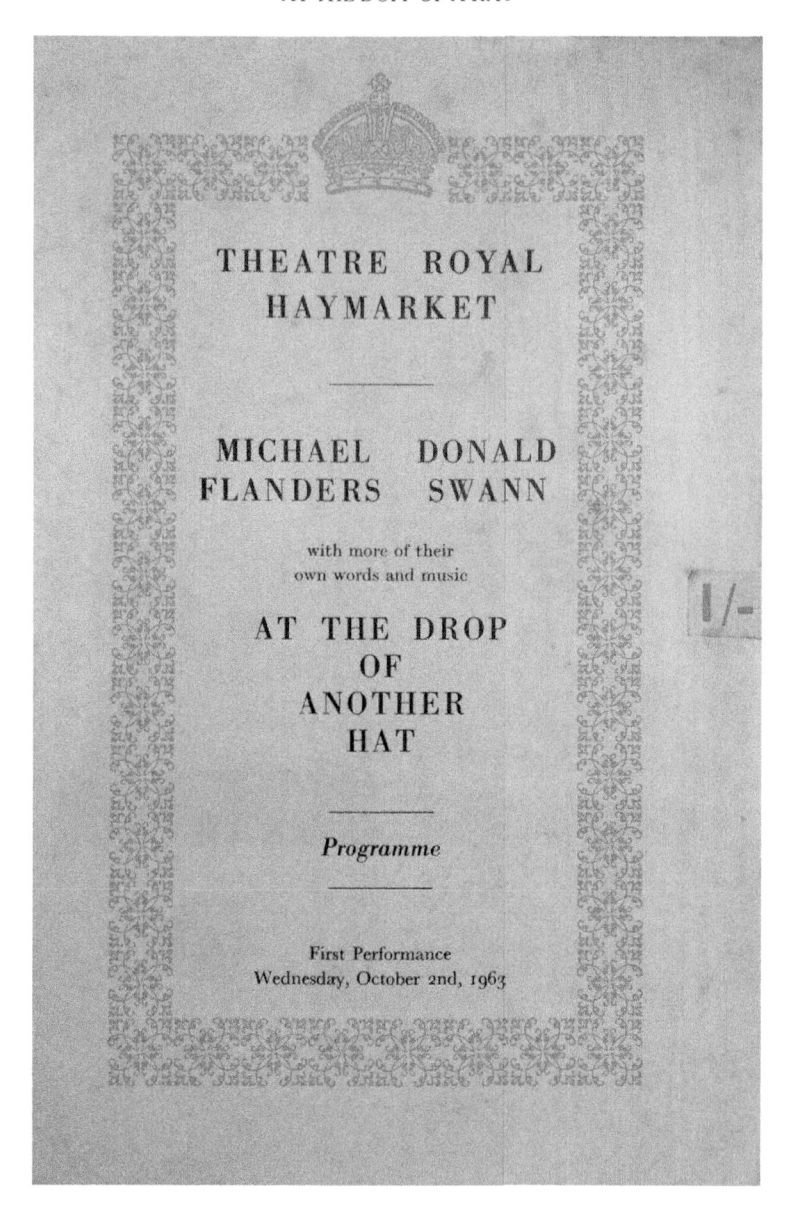

First Performance
Wednesday, October 2nd, 1963

1/-

Theatre Royal Haymarket
Programme: price doubled!

The LP of this show was recorded on the 16th and 18th October sixty years ago. Flanders put words to the first track on the first take:

The Country, the country
The country gets you down
There's nothing like the country
To make you like the town[325]

~~ with which this writer wholeheartedly agrees.

Flanders and Swann appeared along with Tommy Steele in the Royal Variety Performance which was staged on 4th November at the Prince of Wales Theatre. Sibley commented "I remember these two unlikely stars: the bulky, bearded Flanders, who (as a polio sufferer) was in a wheelchair and the slight, bespectacled Swann hunched over the piano keyboard - tearing up the theatre![326] Those were the days.

In 1963 the Old Vic Company (since 1914 *the Home of Shakespeare in London*) gave its last performance in the Waterloo Road. The company was dissolved; the Old Vic

---

[325] Berger, Leon: *Hat-Tricks: guide to the songs*
[326] http://briansibleysblog.blogspot.com/2008/02/who-says-nostalgia-isnt-what-it-was.html

theatre became the temporary home of the new National Theatre. On 15th June at 10.05 p.m. the BBC marked the event with the programme *Farewell to the Vic* for which Flanders provided the commentary. Looking back on the story of a remarkable theatre - among other icons of the British theatre - were Michael Benthall, Richard Burton, Edith Evans, John Gielgud, Alec Guinness, Tyrone Guthrie, Ralph Richardson, Tommy Steele and Sybil Thorndike.[327] You can watch this historic programme on YouTube.[328] It was a Monitor[329] presentation.

---

[327] *https://*genome.ch.bbc.co.uk/schedules/service_bbc_television_servic e/1963-06-15

[328] https://www.youtube.com/watch?v=NvjfMDOZ-2k

[329] BBC arts programme launched 1958

CHAPTER EIGHT
1964 DOWN UNDER

In January, Flanders was awarded an OBE in the New Year Honours.

Then on Sunday the 19th he appeared in the evening at the Royal Festival Hall as narrator in the first public performance of *Twelve Letters* based on Hilaire Belloc's *A Moral Alphabet*:[330] a series of moral poems for children This was broadcast on Radio 3 on Monday 9th February.

Tuesday 10th March, and again one week later, at 2.40 p.m., the Home Service broadcast two talks by Flanders on *Three's Company:* the opera which we noted earlier. Later on Monday 23rd March at 10.50 p.m. and for each of the other weekdays, Flanders and Swann presented *The Man for Others* on television in which they described the events leading up to the crucifixion of Christ: among other things they played the very controversial carol *Friday Morning* by Sydney Carter.

---

[330] jstor.org/stable/950720

On the way to the Palace to collect the OBE

Evidentially, by now Flanders was a highflyer. Accordingly, he was invited to provide the commentary for *Supersonic*; a documentary which was broadcast on 31st March at 9.25 p.m. A handful of men were thinking of making a passenger aircraft to break the sound barrier and in 1959 real work began. The French and the British worked in partnership to save time and money. In 1962 a model of the aircraft was shown at Farnborough Air Show and it was named *Concorde*.[331] America became interested, and not wanting to be left behind, began designing their own sound breaking passenger aircraft. This documentary was mostly made up of interviews with the chief personnel involved in designing, testing and investigating the construction of this supersonic aircraft.[332]

Then, Flanders was the television presenter of *A Gala Performance*; in fifteen episodes over seven seasons between 1965[333] and 1974. His last appearance was on 12th April 1974. He introduced two international stars from the world of opera, Bulgarian bass Nicolai Ghiaurov and English soprano Catherine Wilson.[334] A month later, on

---

[331] Note the spelling!
[332] https://www.acmi.net.au/works/73380--supersonic/
[333] https://genome.ch.bbc.co.uk/schedules/service_bbc_one_london/1965-12-24
[334]

Thursday 20th May he was a guest panellist on BBC's popular and light hearted classical music quiz *Face the Music*; along with his chum Joyce Grenfell and the great Bernard Levin.[335] He appeared on the programme again on Thursday 24th June.

It was suggested that in the 50's and 60's the most sophisticated musical duo in England were Flanders and Swann; with their internationally acclaimed revue. So, it came about that in 1964 the pair went to Australia: they wowed theatre goers wherever they went and enjoyed a sell-out season at Sydney's Theatre Royal.[336] They toured four cities in Australia (and had their children with them),[337] five in New Zealand (at J. C. Williamson Theatres) *and* Hong Kong.

The pair were interviewed in their dressing room in Sydney. They noted that their song about Charles de Gaulle aroused little reaction. Swann commented that they had thought of a title for their third show – *The Hat Trick*: alas it never happened.[338]

---

https://genome.ch.bbc.co.uk/schedules/service_bbc_one_london/1974-04-12

[335]

https://www.imdb.com/title/tt1589718/fullcredits?ref_=tt_ov_st_sm

[336] https://mosmanartgallery.org.au/events/cabaret-in-the-day-glorious-mud-second-show

[337] https://www.nfsa.gov.au/latest/binny-lum-and-stars

The *Australian Jewish Herald* trumpeted their arrival: 'A two man show that (1) took the Edinburgh festival by surprise and (2) took London 2 years and 5 months to get over)' was coming to the Comedy Theatre, Melbourne. The Herald continued 'they should prove hilariously funny to Australians and a change from the usual gag-men of show business.'[339] They were at the Comedy Theatre from the 29th August for three weeks.[340] In Melbourne, Flanders told his audience "Here we are: everything is completely different: Perry Mason is on a Tuesday."[341]

While in Melbourne they were interviewed by the great Binny Lum[342] (she died in 2012 and was known for her friendly, conversational style).[343] Her programmes were popular for their interviews with diverse Australian and international personalities.

---

[338] *Swann Song,* The Bulletin, 28th November 1964
[339] https://trove.nla.gov.au/newspaper/article/265922179?searchTerm=Michael%20Flanders
[340] https://www.nla.gov.au/sites/default/files/blogs/_refresh_01-2015_prompt_-_jc_williamson_-_general_-_may_2017.pdf
[341] Swann, Donald: *Op. cit* , p. 178
[342] https://www.nfsa.gov.au/latest/binny-lum-and-stars
[343] https://soundcloud.com/nfsaaustralia/flanders-and-swann-interviewed

Melbourne flyer

They continued 28th September – 3rd October at His Majesty's Theatre on Queen Street, Auckland;[344] which

---

[344] https://natlib.govt.nz/records/23020668?search%5Bi%5D%5Bname_authority_id%5D=-239702&search%5Bpath%5D=items

was demolished in 1987: at the time one councillor described it as 'a rat-infested dump.'[345]

Later in New Zealand they appeared in:

Hamilton

Palmerston North

12th - 17th October Grand Opera House[346] Wellington

21st - 24th October Theatre Royal, Christchurch[347]

30th October Her Majesty's Theatre, Adelaide

9th November Her Majesty's Theatre, Brisbane[348]

16th November 1964 Theatre Royal, Sydney

---

[345] https://timespanner.blogspot.com/2015/10/aucklands-theatre-on-haymarket-his.html

[346] Now The State Opera House

[347] Now the Isaac Theatre Royal

[348] Demolished 23rd October 1983

The magnificent and historic

Theatre Royal Christchurch

The Sydney programme (1)

THEATRE ROYAL
SYDNEY

J. C. WILLIAMSON THEATRES LTD.

presents

For a season of four weeks only, commencing on MONDAY, NOVEMBER 16, 1964

AT THE DROP OF A HAT

SONG OF REPRODUCTION

ELEPHANT

GREENSLEEVES

THE YOUTH OF THE HEART (lyric by Sydney Carter)

THE GASMAN COMETH

AN ILL WIND (music by Mozart)

SEA FEVER

SLOW TRAIN

A GNU

SONGS FOR OUR TIME

—— Interval of 15 minutes ——

ALL GALL

FIRST AND SECOND LAW

IN THE BATH

A TRANSPORT OF DELIGHT

TRIED BY THE CENTRE COURT

MISALLIANCE

KOKORAKI

MADEIRA, M'DEAR

HIPPOPOTAMUS SONG

★ Music by Donald Swann

★ Words by Michael Flanders

The Sydney programme (2)

The Sydney flyer

Swann recalled that while they were in Hong Kong, they appeared at the Civic Theatre which employed thirteen Chinese stage managers. Flanders asked one of them to bring him a glass of water during the show; it failed to materialise: They asked why. The reply was "Glass of Water Fellow not come."[349]

---

[349] Swann, Donald. Op. cit. p. 180

The Australian LP

While they were away, on Wednesday 14th October at 5.30 p.m., BBC One broadcast *Part-Time Heroes* for which Flanders was the narrator. This was a documentary film about the *Royal National Lifeboat Institution*: illustrating the fact that no other country in the world has such an effective organisation for the saving of life at sea as Britain. The film set out to show something of the scope and methods of the life-boat service and reconstructed two actual incidents: (1) the rescue of three fishermen off the coast of North Wales and (2) a fire on board a coastal ship.

CHAPTER NINE
ON TOP AGAIN

On 1st December 1964, Dobson Books[350] published[351] a book of poems by Flanders aimed at a younger audience. It was *Creatures Great and Small* with illustrations by Marcello Minale.[352] It featured brief humorous verses introducing the characteristics of a variety of animals ('the walrus lives on icy floes and unsuspecting eskimos').

Creatures Great and Small

---

[350] An eccentric, left-wing outfit based in Kensington Church Street
[351] Published in the US in 1965
[352] World-renowned Italian designer, writer and former international oarsman

Feb '65

PALACE THEATRE
WATFORD

Under the Patronage of the Watford Corporation

SIDNEY CROOKE : BEN HAWTHORNE
ESME HAND : LINDA JAMES
MICHAEL KNOWLES : RUTH LLEWELLYN
MIKE PULLEN

and

JAMES & GILDA PERRY

in

"HELLO WATFORD GOODBYE"

PROGRAMME SIXPENCE

Hello Watford Goodbye

1965

Although not billed on the front of the programme, on Friday 5th February[353] Flanders and Swann appeared for one night in the revue *Hello Watford Goodbye* at the town's Palace Theatre; still today the *Home Of Great Theatre*. This was a revue prior to the theatre's closure before refurbishment and subsequent re-opening as a civic theatre. Among those appearing with them was Jimmy Perry who went on to fame and fortune as co-author of *Dad's Army*.

On Friday 6th August, Flanders appeared in *Let's Find Out* on the Light Programme at 7.31 p.m. in which four teenagers asked questions of Lord Soper[354] and Flanders in a programme chaired by Peter Haigh (a popular announcer in the years after the War).

Later in the year, Flanders and Swann then appeared again in the UK *At the Drop of Another Hat*. First from the 6th to the 11th September as part of the festivities

---

[353] https://www.yumpu.com/en/document/read/8377773/palace-theatre-watford-full-list-of-productions-doolleecom
[354] Methodist minister, Socialist and pacifist

celebrating the newly opened Yvonne Arnaud Theatre, Guildford[355] (of which their chum Laurier Lister was the first director). They then proceeded to the New Theatre Oxford on the 13th where Lionel Hampden interviewed them on ATV on the 14th. They went on to the Theatre Royal Brighton for the 20th.[356]

Sunday 3rd October Flanders and Swann appeared in *The Lively Arts* on the Home Service at 4.00 p.m. with an alas unspecified new song.

---

[355] It had opened on 2nd June

[356] https://m.imdb.com/name/nm0281141/otherworks?ref_=nmbio_sa_1

AT THE DOFF OF A HAT

NEW THEATRE
OXFORD

Proprietors: THE OXFORD THEATRE COMPANY LIMITED
Chairman: S. C. DORRILL, M.B.E.
Managing Director: JOHN DORRILL
Manager: T. S. ELSTON

WEEK commencing MONDAY, SEPTEMBER 13th, 1965
Monday to Friday at 7.30   Saturday at 5.0 and 8.0

★ ★ ★

Michael   **Donald**
FLANDERS   **SWANN**
with more of their own words and music

AT THE DROP OF ANOTHER HAT

Box Office (Manager: R. Mossford) Tel. 44544-44545. Open Daily 10 a.m. to 7.30 p.m.
PRICES OF ADMISSION
Stalls and Circle 10/6, 9/6, 8/6, 7/6; Balcony 4/-, Unres. 2/6

The management reserve the right to refuse admission, also to make any alteration in the cast which may be rendered necessary by illness or other unavoidable causes
Photographing in this Theatre is forbidden

ROVER — LAND-ROVER — VAUXHALL
COXETERS of OXFORD
Telephone 42275/6

New Theatre, Oxford
September 1965

On 29th September, the show moved on to Shaftesbury Avenue's Globe Theatre[357] where they ran until 19th February 1966.

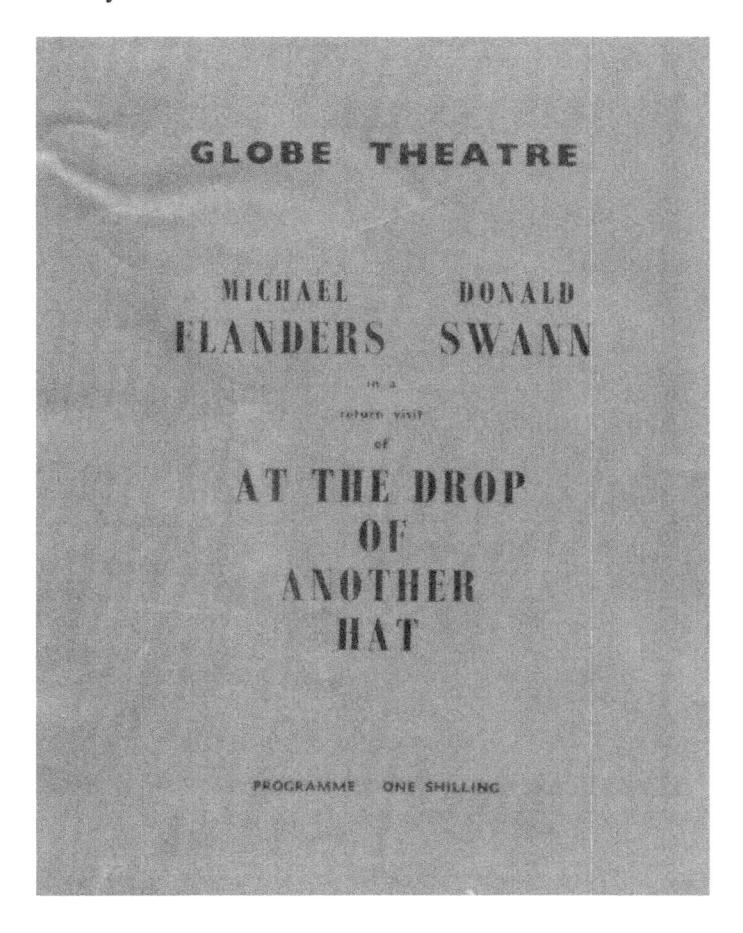

The Globe programme

---

[357] Since 1994, The Gielgud Theatre

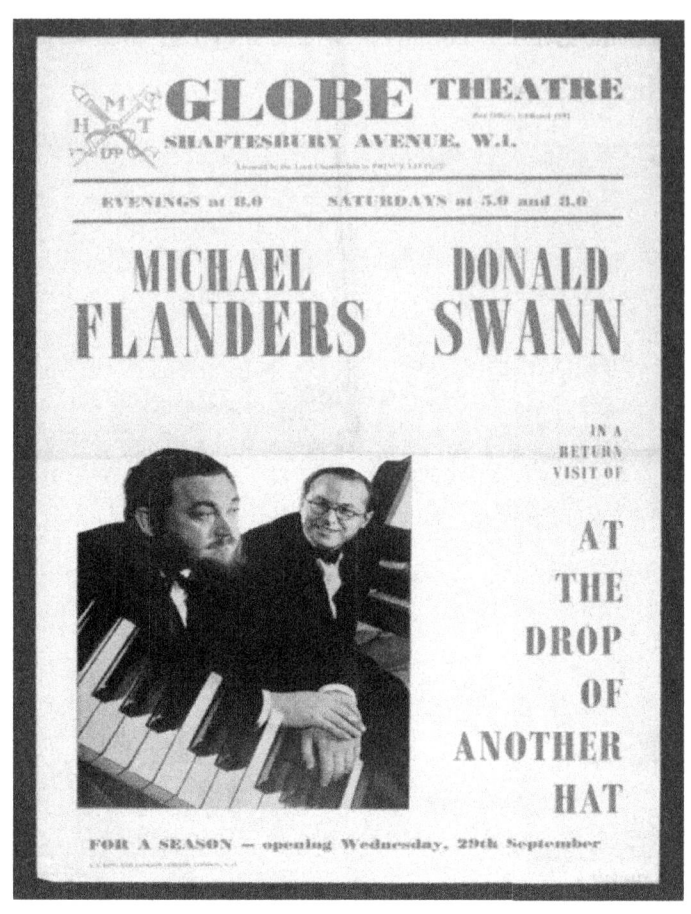

The Globe Flyer

Sunday 10th October, Flanders and Swann appeared on the *Eamonn Andrews Show*. This was a late-night chat and music programme from ABC Weekend TV hosted by the genial Irishman: allegedly with Eamonn sweating buckets over his "famous, frank and funny guests."[358] It was recorded earlier that evening at Teddington Studios.[359] *The Eamonn Andrews Show* was the first real British attempt to repeat the success of American chat shows:[360] it ran for five years on Sunday evenings so must have been judged a moderate success.

1966

Sunday 30th January at 7.35 p.m. on the Light Programme Flanders and Swann appeared on *Startime*. Ralph Reader[361] introduced entertainment on record of some of the world's greatest artistes.

---

[358] https://nostalgiacentral.com/television/tv-by-decade/tv-shows-1960s/eamonn-andrews-show/

[359] Run by Pinewood – demolished 2016

[360] https://genome.ch.bbc.co.uk/schedules/service_bbc_one_london/1966-09-06

[361] **Born in Crewkerne.** British actor, theatrical producer and songwriter: famous for the gang show

On Friday 4th March 1966, Flanders introduced two ballet dancers - Nadia Nerina and Christopher Gable - in two excerpts from *Cinderella*: *The Broom Dance* and *the pas de deux*[362] from the Ballroom Scene. On 22nd April on the same programme Flanders introduced Margot Fonteyne and Attilio Labis in *The Shadow Dance* from Act I of *Ondine*.

Tuesday 6th September at 10.50 p.m. (and on 29th August 1967 at 5.15 p.m.)[363] saw the broadcast of *Fact Not Fiction: Take Another Note* a thirty-five-minute television special with Flanders as the presenter. This was a fascinating programme in which collectors of unusual musical instruments talked to Flanders about their hobby.

At 1.10 p.m. on the Home Service on Monday 27th December, in a pre-recorded broadcast, Flanders was the castaway on the popular radio show *Desert Island Discs*.[364] Interviewed by the show's originator Roy Plumley he said that his choice of book on the island would be a blank book together with pencils and that his luxury item would be a horn; presumably French. Among the tracks that he chose were *Soirées musicales - Tarantella* by Benjie

---

[362] Dance duet in which two dancers perform ballet steps together
[363] https://genome.ch.bbc.co.uk/4b62499a24394de2a60de2e5da4849d9
[364] https://www.bbc.co.uk/programmes/p009y3r8

Britten and Richard Burton's *Camelot*. Flanders and Swann had of course been joint guests on the programme together in 1958.[365]

---

[365] https://www.bbc.co.uk/programmes/p009y8fg

CHAPTER TEN
1966
BACK TO AMERICA - AU REVOIR

So, unknown to many at the time, 1966 marked the beginning of the end. Flanders and Swann returned to the US for a ten-theatre tour before once again playing New York. On Saturday 5th November 1966[366] *Billboard* magazine reported that when Flanders and Swann opened *At the Drop of Another Hat* in New York on Monday 26th December they would have spent three months on the road; having opened to rave reviews in Boston on Monday 26th September.

---

[366] https://books.google.co.uk/books?id=LSkEAAAAMBAJ&pg=PA24&lpg=PA24&dq=shubert+theatre+flanders+and+swann&source=bl&ots=PM-9GBjqB7&sig=ACfU3U3u5-SVjmHGU3mVjWv33SEZYnbEIA&hl=en&sa=X&ved=2ahUKEwjP-qvTjdb7AhVLe8AKHdwTBUk4ChDoAXoECAQQAw#v=onepage&q=shubert%20theatre%20flanders%20and%20swann&f=false

Flanders and Swann appeared at:

26th September – 8th October: Wilbur Theatre, Boston, MA

Murat Theatre, Indianapolis, IN

Louisville, KY

Detroit, MI

Shubert Theatre, Cincinnati, OH

2nd - 5th November: Shubert Theatre, New Haven, CT

7th – 12th November: The Locust, Philadelphia, PE

14th - 16th November: National Theatre, Washington, DC[367]

28th November - 10th December: O'Keefe Theatre, Toronto

12th - 17th December: Hanna Theatre, Cleveland, OH

---

[367] Closed 1980: demolished 1982

Wilbur Theatre, Boston

flyer

Shubert Theatre, New Haven

promo

WEDNESDAY, NOVEMBER 2 thru SATURDAY, NOVEMBER 5 at 8:30
Matinee Saturday at 2:30

ALEXANDER H. COHEN

presents

MICHAEL FLANDERS DONALD SWANN

with more of their
own words and music

AT THE DROP OF ANOTHER HAT

Associate Producer Designed by
Sidney Lanier **Ralph Alswang**

Original Cast Album, Angel Records

THE PROGRAMME

THE GAS-MAN COMETH

FROM OUR BESTIARY

BILBO'S SONG (lyric by J. R. R. Tolkien)

BY AIR

SLOW TRAIN

THERMODYNAMIC DUO

SLOTH

P** P* B**** B** D******

LOS OLIVIDADOS

IN THE DESERT

New Haven: part of their offering

National Theatre, Washington

flyer

AT THE DOFF OF A HAT

National Theatre, Washington

programme

AT THE DOFF OF A HAT

Booth Theatre, New York
The final programme

Flanders and Swann opened at the Booth Theatre on Time Square, New York on Tuesday 27th December. They played through Sunday 9th April 1967: one hundred and five performances.[368] They won some of the season's best notices.[369] George Oppenheimer[370] noted, "In a season largely devoid of merriment and mainly dedicated to mediocrity, the bearded Flanders and the bespectacled Swann provide an oasis; complete with palms that ache from applauding."[371]

John Chapman in the *New York Daily News* praised their 'civilized proceedings'; but one reviewer found them faintly smug. He thought that a full evening of them was tiresome:[372] well, there is no accounting for taste. *The*

---

[368] http://www.iankitching.me.uk/humour/hippo/career.html

[369] https://books.google.co.uk/books?id=6NBiAwAAQBAJ&pg=PA403&lpg=PA403&dq=Flanders+and+swann+%2B+booth+theatre&source=bl&ots=2m_CWSVwmv&sig=ACfU3U2KPWUMKsI0j39wG5DjmZolAooBAQ&hl=en&sa=X&ved=2ahUKEwjOzLSi3fn7AhUOEcAKHZhnDp44KBDoAXoECAQQAg#v=onepage&q=Flanders%20and%20swann%20%2B%20booth%20theatre&f=false

[370] Drama critic for *Newsday*

[371] https://www.filmedlivemusicals.com/drop-another-hat.html

[372] https://books.google.co.uk/books?id=6NBiAwAAQBAJ&pg=PA403&lpg=PA403&dq=Flanders+and+swann+%2B+booth+theatre&source=bl&ots=2m_CWSVwmv&sig=ACfU3U2KPWUMKsI0j39wG5DjmZolAooBAQ&hl=en&sa=X&ved=2ahUKEwjOzLSi3fn7AhUOEcAKHZhnDp44KBDoAXoECAQQAg#v=onepage&q=Flanders%20and%20swann%20%2B%20booth%20theatre&f=false

Times said 'Head out for the Booth where the new year is already happy.'[373] The *New York Post* remarked 'that you could not find a better way of having a more delightful evening'.[374] The grandiosely named *New York World Journal Tribune*[375] added that 'off stage or on, there are not two more erudite and affable companions.'[376]

While in New York, Flanders was introduced to Bernard Jacobson[377] by Max Rudolf.[378] Jacobson remarked that he had seen Flanders in 1964 when he narrated *Twelve Letters*.[379] Jacobson recalled that the Flanders were

---

[373]
https://books.google.co.uk/books?id=CSkEAAAAMBAJ&pg=PA24&lpg=PA24&dq=at+the+drop+of+a+hat+flanders+and+swann&source=bl&ots=6TNCZbn9Ss&sig=ACfU3U2t2HDTPenNZK_3_CKco2vAROktpQ&hl=en&sa=X&ved=2ahUKEwjS3q7Lv5r9AhX7REEAHbrmCCU4RhDoAXoECBMQAw#v=onepage&q=at%20the%20drop%20of%20a%20hat%20flanders%20and%20swann&f=false

[374]
https://books.google.co.uk/books?id=CSkEAAAAMBAJ&pg=PA24&lpg=PA24&dq=at+the+drop+of+a+hat+flanders+and+swann&source=bl&ots=6TNCZbn9Ss&sig=ACfU3U2t2HDTPenNZK_3_CKco2vAROktpQ&hl=en&sa=X&ved=2ahUKEwjS3q7Lv5r9AhX7REEAHbrmCCU4RhDoAXoECBMQAw#v=onepage&q=at%20the%20drop%20of%20a%20hat%20flanders%20and%20swann&f=false

[375] Closed May 1967 – after just nine months

[376] Op. cit

[377] His career included spells as recording executive; music critic of the *Chicago Daily News*; artistic director and adviser to international orchestras in Holland; and visiting professor at Roosevelt University's Chicago Musical College

[378] German conductor

staying at the Buckingham Hotel[380] and remembers that the two of them held a weekly soirée there for anyone connected with the British theatre who happened to be in New York: among others Jacobson met Lynn Redgrave and Paul Scofield at these gatherings. Later in 1967 the Flanders invited Jacobson to visit them at their summer retreat at West Dennis on Cape Cod.[381]

1967

Flanders' and Swann's collaboration ended on Broadway on 9th April 1967. Swann remembers that Alex Cohen tried hard to persuade them to carry on: but Swann resolved that the 'show must end.'[382] The decision to stop playing the *Hat* shows was chiefly his: he felt their collaboration was impeding his claims to be a serious

---

[379] https://books.google.co.uk/books?id=o3ADCwAAQBAJ&pg=PA72&lpg=PA72&dq=flanders+and+swann+%2B+cincinnati+%2B+1966&source=bl&ots=teN1LFaGkP&sig=ACfU3U2rZETToRGzbIqxvpaO7YCZWGsdNg&hl=en&sa=X&ved=2ahUKEwj-xIzwkov8AhVWi1wKHX6bAR0Q6AF6BAgWEAM#v=onepage&q=flanders%20and%20swann%20%2B%20cincinnati%20%2B%201966&f=false

[380] Now The Quin (Hilton): built as a Beaux-Arts style building

[381] It boasts a mile-long, wheel chair-accessible beach whose conditions make it ideal for kite-flying and windsurfing

[382] Swann, Donald: Op. cit. p. 181

composer. As John Barber said "They broke all the rules by performing so long and then broke them all again by refusing the calls to return."[383]

Flanders was keen to carry on and he missed the show until the end of his days; it had become an essential part of him.[384] However, the two men remained friends and continued to collaborate from time to time[385] for the show had put them both in the Hall of Fame.[386] They were a real pair and Flanders' use of his wheelchair was most theatrical.[387] Swann recalled that Flanders would put his hand on Swann's stool and that this created an intimacy between them on stage.

Saturday 30th December and again on 4th August 1971 Flanders appeared in *A Choice of Paperbacks* broadcast on Radio 4 at 9.00 p.m. Introduced by Cliff Michelmore; fellow contributors were among others, Brian Rix, Jo Grimond MP and Shirley Williams MP. Flanders gave readings from books that were funny and scary.

---

[383] https://www.johnbarber.com/flanders-swann/
[384] Swann, Donald. Op. cit. p. 182
[385] https://en.wikipedia.org/wiki/Michael_Flanders
[386] Amiss, John: *Dropping the Hat Again*, Radio 2 documentary, 12th January 1997
[387] Op. cit. p. 185

CHAPTER ELEVEN
TELEVISION

Saturday 9th December 1967 at 7.00 p.m. on Radio 4 Flanders and Swann appeared alongside a collection of well-known personalities including David Frost and Sammy Davis Jr. in *What's so funny about our pets: or It's Enough to Make a Cat Laugh*. It was a comedy anthology; one which would have required no acting on their part whatsoever.

The pair reunited shortly after closing in New York to tape *At the Drop of Another Hat* for CBS. It was filmed at the Ed Sullivan Theater at 1697 Broadway. It was broadcast on 18th December 1967 and was released on VHS.[388] The footage is currently available on YouTube under the erroneous title *The Only Flanders and Swann Video*. The actual recording took over seven hours. The duo were reportedly frustrated by the stops and starts to adjust lighting and angles: the audience were likely

---

[388] https://www.imdb.com/title/tt1736544/fullcredits?ref_=ttrel_ql_1

exhausted.[389] One imagines that they were glad that the hat had indeed dropped at the end.

It was in fact not their only televised show. An hour-long version of *At the Drop of a Hat,* based on both the New York and the touring versions of the show, was filmed for television on 10th May 1962 in Studio 4 of the BBC Television Centre at White City. This was a co-production of Alexander H. Cohen, Talent Associates - Paramount Limited, the Festival of the Performing Arts[390] and the BBC.[391] At the time of the taping, Flanders was performing as The Storyteller in *The Caucasian Chalk Circle* at the Aldwych Theatre; the recording was made on a day-off from his performances. A week after the taping, on 16th May, Flanders wrote to Alex Cohen noting "The telerecording went excellently and everybody was pleased - even Donald and I; though of course we have not seen it yet." Flanders told Cohen that the duo enjoyed working with producer David Susskind,[392] describing him

---

[389] https://www.filmedlivemusicals.com/blog/up-close-with-flanders-swann

[390] A short-lived cultural television program sponsored by the New Jersey Standard Oil Company

[391] https://www.filmedlivemusicals.com/at-the-drop-hat.html

[392] Produced numerous television programmes, including *Circle Theater* (1955–63) and *Dupont Show of the Month* (1957–64), but he became best known as host of the talk shows *Open End* (1958–67) and *The David Susskind Show* (1967–86); for which he won many

as his "usual charming, stimulating and enthusiastic self." Flanders also noted that director Harry Carlisle "made everything as easy for us as possible." *At the Drop of a Hat* aired in New York City and Washington D.C. on 22nd May 1962; with a repeat on 27th May.

The programme was filmed before an invited audience.[393] A few weeks before the taping, Flanders and Swann sent Cohen a telegram urgently requesting that he confirm with the BBC that the contracts did not include rights for the BBC to air the tape and only included "local American transmission." In mid to late May 1962, Cohen and Flanders exchanged several letters regarding concerns over a British broadcast. Flanders had three issues in mind; fair renumeration, impact on future audiences and impact on future tapings with the BBC.

According to Flanders, the BBC and ITV had approached the duo "several times to do the show for them." In his 16th May letter to Cohen, Flanders noted that the financial renumeration British networks could offer was "not as great as on your side," and that "…we in Equity[394] have just emerged from a seven months strike

---

awards
[393] https://www.filmedlivemusicals.com/blog/up-close-with-flanders-swann
[394] **Founded 1930:** the trade union for the performing arts and

against ITV to establish the principal of payment by potential size of audience." Flanders suggested that a leading actor in a half hour play could expect "at least $1,500 for a single performance with further sums for residuals and showing outside the UK." In a second letter dated 17th May, Flanders once again requested that Cohen arrange for a higher percentage of net profits.

Regarding audience, Flanders stated that "Talent Associates will no doubt argue that showing the tape of the show will create further demand," but he was concerned that showing *At the Drop of a Hat* on television would limit their audience, as their act did not change like a variety act, and was more set like a musical. In spite of this statement, as the *New York Times* obituarist noted, a Flanders and Swann performance really had to be seen to be believed, let alone appreciated, especially since Flanders was at all times in a wheelchair.[395] It commented that Flanders knowingly delivered satirical wisdom from the confines of his trademark wheelchair *and that* it was impossible to forget their wry comic observations of modern life.[396]

---

entertainment industries
[395] https://www.nytimes.com/1975/04/16/archives/michael-flanders-is-dead-at-53-humoriststar-of-drop-of-a-hat.html
[396] https://www.sidmouthherald.co.uk/things-to-do/20475218.glories-

In his 17th May letter, Flanders noted that the recording had been specifically made for American audiences and that as a result of the back and forth, the BBC might not be so willing to provide facilities "all over again" for a British version. Flanders indicated that he was willing to have the show broadcast in the UK; but only for a better fee.

On 8th June 1962, Cohen confirmed with Flanders that Robert Fenn from Music Corporation of America had negotiated $5000 for the British rights. A week later, on 13th June, Fenn confirmed the deal. He noted "We found the contract so complicated that I felt bound to ask advice from the New York office" Poor chap! The British recording was broadcast on television on Thursday 21st June 1962 at 7.55 p.m.

---

music-hall/

CHAPTER TWELVE
WRITER AND BROADCASTER

Flanders was a team captain in *Call My Bluff* from 1966-1967:[397] he was the first and only game show host in a wheelchair.[398] The programme was a successful British panel game show based on the American show of the same name by Goodson-Toddman Productions (who produced some of the longest-running game shows in US television history). A word was given and each member of one team would give one of three possible definitions for that word. Only one of those definitions would be correct. If the other team chose the correct definition, they scored one point; however, if they were wrong the bluffing team got the point.

Flanders was a composer for two episodes of *Before the Fringe* which was shown over fourteen episodes in two series (8+6) on BBC One and later BBC Two between 1967 and 1968. The programme attempted to showcase some of the talent in vogue in pre-*Before the*

---

[397] https://british-game-show.fandom.com/wiki/Call_My_Bluff
[398] http://www.ukgameshows.com/ukgs/Michael_Flanders

Fringe revues and before the graduates of the *Cambridge Footlights* took the genre by storm. It sought to demonstrate that the medium had been a much gentler, broader affair.[399]

Sponsored by John Harvey and Sons Ltd,[400] *The Best Sherry in the World*[401]/[402] was broadcast in 1967 with Flanders (more famous for his knowledge of madeira!) as narrator. And there is little record of it![403]

Friday 21st July at 10.35 p.m. Flanders and Swann appeared on *Music through Midnight* (which today would probably be Music thru Midnite); this was the programme (which later) was the last one broadcast on the old Light Programme.

Sunday 6th August at 9.35 p.m. on BBC Two Flanders appeared in *Bauhütte 63*. He was the narrator in an award-winning film about the continuing work of a German mediaeval guild workshop and the restoration of the evangelical Lutheran Freiburg Cathedral[404] in Saxony: it is famed for its great organ.

---

[399] https://www.wikiwand.com/en/Before_the_Fringe
[400] https://www2.bfi.org.uk/films-tv-people/4ce2b6d9801e2
[401] https://archives.bristol.gov.uk/records/BROFA/0134
[402] https://www.imdb.com/title/tt4685236/fullcredits/?ref_=tt_ql_1
[403] https://www.imdb.com/title/tt4685236/
[404] Built around 1180: so older than the author's own house

Friday 8th December - and a week later - at 7.00 p.m. on Radio 4, Flanders and Swann appeared on *Who? What? Where? When?* Yet another quiz programme: this time hosted by Ken Sykora:[405] in which the host tested the panel with the help of sounds, voices, and music from the BBC Sound Archives.

Flanders appeared on Wednesday 20th December (just before closedown) at 10.52 p.m. on BBC's *Viewpoint*[406] (once more as a narrator) in *A Christmas Cartoon: Det hande sig ar noll*. This was an experimental film from Sweden with animated children's drawings of the Fall of Man and the Birth of Christ. We do not know if the "experiment" was a success! This was broadcast three months later on 28th March 1968 on BBC at 9.05 p.m.[407] presumably as an Easter cartoon.

Saturday 30th December at 7.00 p.m. on Radio 4, Flanders and Swann appeared in an anthology in *What's so funny about our transport (it's driving that driving me mad)*. The great Bob Newhart[408] was another contributor.

---

[405] Host of the Guitar Club
[406] Long running flagship religious series
[407] https://www.bbc.co.uk/schedules/p00fzl6p/1968/03/28
[408] Deadpan actor and comedian

Flanders was the narrator along with various voice actors - on a Decca LP *The Makers of History: Elizabeth the Great* - celebrating the life of Elizabeth the First.

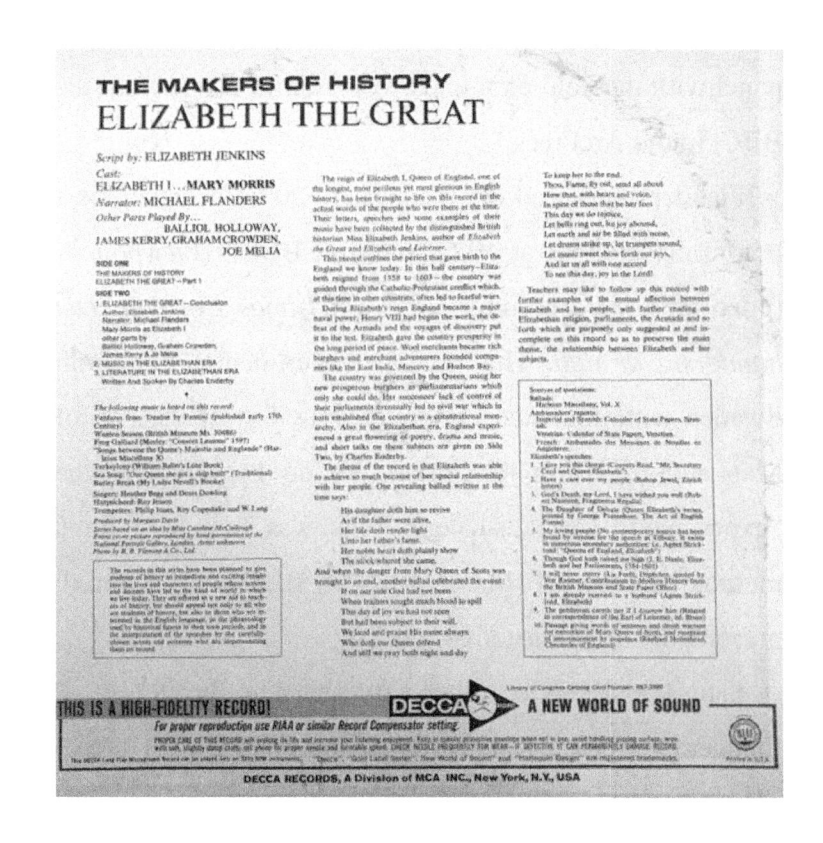

Elizabeth the Great LP

1968

Saturday 27th January was marked by a three-minute appearance by Flanders on *Dee Time*. Fronted by the allegedly charismatic Simon Dee[409] this programme purported to be entertainment; it included interviews with big shots in the music industry. Dee eventually became a national laughing stock and went to prison. Flanders appearance went out at 6.25 p.m. and one wonders what he thought he was doing on a show fronted by such a cretin.

On Tuesday 19th March at 10.30 p.m. on BBC's arts-based documentary series *Omnibus*[410] Flanders introduced excerpts from the widely acclaimed New York revue *Julius Monk's Plaza 9*[411] with Liz Sheridan, Rex Robbins, Terry O'Mara, Alex Wipf and Mary Louise Wilson.

Later on Thursday 28th March at 9.05 p.m. *Fifty Years of the R.A.F.* was celebrated. Flanders narrated an overview of the major events of the *Battle of Britain*,[412] including a discussion between battle pilots Group

---

[409] Cyril Nicholas Henty-Dodd
[410] Successor to *Monitor*
[411] The Rendezvous Room (Plaza 9) at the Plaza Hotel
[412] https://www.bbc.co.uk/programmes/p0095vws

Captain Sir Douglas Bader and Wing Commander Paddy Barthropp[413] about the significance of the fight.

Monday 27th May at 7.00 p.m. on Radio Four, together with (retired) opera singer and broadcaster David Franklin, Flanders challenged two other contestants in the long running and popular show *My Music!*

At 10.25 p.m. on Tuesday 11th June the *Omnibus* programme broadcast *The Seven Deadly Sins*: An Operatic Enquiry; written by Flanders. This writer ponders the nature of an 'operatic enquiry'!

Monday 29th July Flanders appeared on Radio Four in *What's So Funny About Our Sport?* at 7.00 p.m. This was a comedy anthology written and introduced by Basil Boothroyd who fancied himself as a humorist and (having initially worked as a bank clerk) later wrote for *Punch*. He wrote several similar comic programmes with similar names.

---

[413] https://www.rafmuseum.org.uk/blog/a-full-life-wg-cdr-patrick-paddy-barthropp/

Monday 12th August Flanders appeared in *What's so funny about our glorious past? (Or 1066 and all what?)*. A month later on Monday 26th August Flanders and Swann appeared in *What's so funny about love and marriage? (Or Boy meets Guile*) broadcast on Radio 4 at 7.00 p.m. It must have been funny as it also featured Benny Hill and Roy Hudd among others.

Friday 6th September (repeated a month later) Flanders appeared in *She Wou'd if she Cou'd*[414] on Radio Three at 7.30 p.m. This was an early restoration comedy by English dramatist Sir George Etherege and featured music composed and directed by Donald Swann. It presented a colourfully etched image of London three and a half centuries ago, its inns and arbours, with two men-about-town courting two pert country girls; a flighty county lady and a lustful knight thwarted in their amorous pursuits: a gent from the seedier side of society bragging to no purpose: and a rollicking squire catching a wily servant girl.

The BBC ran a very successful *Scrapbook* series on the Home Service. Leslie Baily had put forward the idea of a radio scrapbook, and was told that they were willing to try one "as an experiment". Freddy Grisewood was

---

[414] https://genome.ch.bbc.co.uk/e52ee918e22845e6ac36ddea46cdbfaf

appointed to turn the pages. It was on 11th December 1933 that Scrapbook set out on its long journey on national radio, each issue being dedicated to a specific year. Flanders took over as narrator on the *Armistice Scrapbook* broadcast Sunday 10th November. He continued until the last programme in May 1974.[415] The experiment clearly worked and he was a *natural* for it. One of its more interesting editions was *Scrapbook for 1941* broadcast on Monday 10th September 1973 at 11.05 a.m. It featured recordings of men and women recalling experiences at home and abroad during a year that marked the nadir of Britain's fortunes in the Second World War; together with music and popular songs of the period.

Tuesday 26th November at 9.05 p.m. on BBC One Flanders was the narrator in *Towards Tomorrow: Time to Kill.* This was an interesting discussion into the increasing spread of leisure time. It was suggested that what the producers called the 'Gospel of Work' is hard to shake off. It suggested that when we get the chance of more free time, many of us shy away. Perhaps we enjoy our time off only because we know it must come to an end. But what will happen when it does not? Professor Dennis Gabor made the extreme suggestion that the age of

---

[415] http://www.suttonelms.org.uk/articles31.html

leisure, if it comes too early, could be as big a potential threat to society as the atom-bomb. It was reported that some Britons already had a four-day week (once again a topical idea in 2023). It was reported that in Lancashire there was already a three-day week and that industrial change would bring more spare time for everybody. The programme asked 'are we ready or will leisure mean more of us seeking refuge in alcohol, drugs, and fantasy?': (well, see what happened during Lockdown). The programme suggested that from new-style educational holiday camps to giant 'fun bubbles' to roll around in, the battle was on to liven people up on the threshold of the age of leisure.

Monday 9th December Flanders appeared in *A Moral Alphabet*[416] at 8.00 p.m. on Radio 3: he was to do so again a year later. He read poetry in this strangely named programme. He clearly enjoyed reading poetry.

During 1968, Flanders appeared at the Queen Elizabeth Hall,[417] London, as the narrator in *The Soldier's Tale*.[418]

---

[416] A series of moral poems for children: here set for voice and quintet by Hilaire Belloc; published in 1899

[417] At the South Bank Centre: built in a brutalist style in 1967 and refurbished in 2018

[418] A mixed-media piece using speech, mime, and dance accompanied by a seven-piece band

Later Flanders appeared in the London Weekend Television production of *No! No! No!* as Judge Gampstrup.

1969

Following that, Flanders appeared as narrator in the BAFTA award nominated documentary *The Behaviour Game*. Broadcast on Wednesday 1st January, it investigated how bad behaviour affects colleagues and the public; and considered the correct way to act towards others.

On Sunday 16th March, Flanders made yet another appeal on *This Week's Good Cause:* this time on behalf of *The Migraine Trust*. This trust had been formed in 1965 to stimulate and finance research into all aspects of this distressing complaint: it is still going strong.

Tuesday 18th March, Flanders and Swann appeared on *As You Like It* on Radio 2 at 9.15 p.m. Their old chum Ian Wallace introduced listeners' requests along with the two great men. Later, on Tuesday 5th August, pianist and broadcaster Joseph Cooper featured Flanders and Swann on the same programme.

Sunday 29th June at 10.30 p.m. on Radio 2 Eric Robinson introduced Flanders and Swann as guests on his show *Eric Robinson (Melodies for you)*. Saturday 26th July at 3.00 p.m. on Radio 4 Flanders appeared on *Weekend Woman's Hour*.

Later on, Flanders was the narrator in the thirteen-part series *The Battle of the Atlantic 1939-45*. This series was broadcast on Radio 4 in summer 1969 and concerned the longest and most complex campaign of the Second World War. It recounted crucial events of the war at sea and was written and produced by John Bridges.[419]

Thursday 25th September on Radio 4 at 7.30 p.m. and again on 9th April 1970 at 9.05 a.m. on Radio 4 Flanders presented a tribute to Gerard Hoffnung. Flanders and many others looked at the life and activities of the artist, musician, eccentric and wit who (having been brought to London to escape the Nazis) had died of a sudden stroke just over ten years earlier; aged just thirty-four and already looking old. It was a programme made for Flanders' own particular genius.

But **the** big television event of the year was the *Royal Family* broadcast on Saturday 21st June. It was the first

---

[419] https://genome.ch.bbc.co.uk/22071c92d3ed43d587c7bf783e0e90a9

documentary offering an intimate portrait of the daily life of the British royal family; drawn from eighteen months of filming within Buckingham Palace, Windsor Castle and Balmoral. The concept behind the documentary was to soften and modernize the royal image. But members of the family, including the Queen, were reportedly dubious about the idea from the start. After its premiere, Buckingham Palace greatly limited the film's circulation.[420]/[421]

The film *was* controversial and will never be broadcast again but its voice-over narration, read by Flanders, carried an authoritative official tone and made an effort to project the perceived importance of the Crown to the country.[422]

Having said that, in a commentary on the film in January 2021, the *Daily Telegraph*[423] opined (not altogether kindly) that *in one terrific moment*, Flanders' commentary (written by Sir Anthony Jay)[424] tells us the

---

[420] https://www.history.com/news/queen-elizabeth-ii-1969-royal-family-documentary

[421] It was re-broadcast again in 1972 *and* 1977 at the time of the Queen's Silver Jubilee

[422] https://letterboxd.com/film/royal-family/

[423] https://www.telegraph.co.uk/tv/0/fascinating-charming-bbcs-royal-family-humanises-windsors-much/

[424] Co-writer of the influential satire *Yes Minister*

Royal family represents a broad range of interests, a broad sweep of society. "The Duchess of Kent, for instance," he says, "is a Yorkshire woman.'" We do not know what Flanders thought of it.

Flanders was narrator for the BBC's thirteen-part series *The Master Chefs*[425/426] directed by Thomas Stobart. This series showed some of the master chefs of Europe preparing dishes in their own restaurants.

Sunday 20th October Flanders appeared once again in a *Moral Alphabet* on Radio 3 at 9.15 p.m. There were the verses by Hilaire Belloc set for voice and quintet spoken by Flanders.

Sunday 30th November Flanders was on Radio 4 at 10.55 a.m. with another appeal for *This Week's Good Cause*. This time the focus was the *National Council for Social Service*. This was a widely representative body which was engaged in co-ordinating and guiding voluntary efforts to provide occupation for the unemployed.

Christmas saw Flanders introduce the Wandsworth School Choir on BBC Two at 10.50 p.m. singing Christmas carols. On Christmas Day itself he appeared on

---

[425] https://www2.bfi.org.uk/films-tv-people/4ce2b9fd22cef

[426] https://www.imdb.com/title/tt23326088/?ref_=nm_flmg_cin_2

Let's go with Cliff at 1.15 p.m. on Radio 4. Why Flanders and Swann (who had retired as a partnership) wanted to associate themselves with Cliff Richard heaven only knows.

1970

Flanders appeared at the May Fair Theatre in a revue, *Ten Years Hard* by Peter Myers. His performance was praised, but the show was not; it closed within a month.[427] The theatre itself was of interest. It opened in 1963 and was situated in the former Candlelight Room of the May Fair Hotel, on Stratton Street, near the famous Berkeley Square. The theatre entrance was situated just to the left of the hotel entrance and its Box Office was just inside the doors. The theatre was converted into a cinema when the hotel was renovated in 2005. Its main use today is for private screenings, conferences and product launches. The stage is still there but is now blocked off and used as office space. A door to the left of the former proscenium arch[428] of the theatre in the cinema still leads to the former stage.

---

[427] https://en.wikipedia.org/wiki/Michael_Flanders
[428] Describes the frame that surrounds a stage space; separating the audience from the stage

Monday 16th March Flanders appeared on *Woman's Hour* on Radio 2 (then at 2.00 p.m.) and read *The Art of Coarse Rugby* by Michael Green.[429] I am not sure how this fitted in with women's tastes. He continued the following day: both editions were presented by Marjorie Anderson.

Sunday 19th April at 10.35 p.m. Flanders again hosted *Omnibus*. In this edition, Kenneth More (the actor who created the part of Jolyon in The Forsyte Saga) discussed his start in the theatrical profession; appearing at the Windmill Theatre, his years in repertory and his rapid rise to stardom. More had become one of the heroic acting figures of the 1950s.

Saturday 25th April, 2nd May and 9th May 1970 on Radio 4 at 3.00 p.m. Flanders appeared again in *Weekend Woman's Hour* as usual at that time presented by Marjorie Anderson. Flanders read *stuff by* T. F. Powys[430] on three occasions.

Tuesday 16th June 1970 at 9.10 p.m. on BBC One Flanders was the narrator in *Europe – A Continent Fit To Live In: Tuesday's Documentary*. This was a special programme for European Conservation Year.

---

[429] He was a British journalist and author of humorous books

[430] British novelist and short-story writer best remembered for his allegorical novel *Mr. Weston's Good Wine*: in which Mr Weston the wine merchant is evidently God

Even then Europe still had some weird and wonderful wildlife; and some remote and unknown wildernesses. In this varied continent, stretching from Iceland to Turkey *and* from Portugal to Russia, flamingos, porcupines, pelicans, bison and polar bears still survived. But for how long? the programme asked appropriately as it was filmed in fourteen countries.

Saturday 22nd August at 2.05 p.m. on Radio 3 on *Afternoon Sequence* among other things Flanders once again narrated Prokofiev's *Peter and the Wolf*.

On several occasions in the autumn of 1970 (first Monday 21st September on BBC Two at 9.20 p.m.) Flanders appeared as the narrator in *Horizon*. Among several there was *Mind the Machine, Water Water* and *the Man who talks to Frogs*. The latter featured the Smithsonian Tropical Research Institute on an island in the middle of the Panama Canal. Here Dr Stanley Rand learnt the language of frogs while investigating their surprisingly complex mating calls. Flanders was just the man for this task.

7th December, Flanders presented *Square Pegs* on *Horizon* on BBC Two: a series that covered science and philosophy. Flanders narrated this programme, which he must have found very interesting, for it investigated some of the testing techniques used in management selection for job applicants.[431] The programme (broadcast at 9.20 p.m.) was one of the *Man and Science* series. It asked what chance do you have of getting a better job? It suggested that applying for one often meant submitting to innumerable tests not only of ability and intelligence but also of personality. It questioned just how valid some of those tests actually were and followed two candidates through their ordeal.[432]

On 27th December 1970 Flanders introduced a special bank holiday edition of *Options* which featured a résumé of what was going on in the arts. This included the Sadler's Wells production of the Cole Porter musical *Kiss Me Kate*; the film of Edith Nesbit's story *The Railway Children* (now regarded as a classic) and the music-hall tradition in the theatre (which was very much a Flanders' passion).

1970 saw Flanders narrate Cláudio Villas-Boas's commentary in *The Tribe That Hides from Man*.[433] Shot

---

[431] https://genome.ch.bbc.co.uk/schedules/service_bbc_two_england/1970-12-07

[432] http://collections-search.bfi.org.uk/web/Details/ChoiceFilmWorks/150080116

[433] https://www2.bfi.org.uk/films-tv-people/4ce2b6a191568

over two years by Adrian Cowell, it was an extraordinary film *and* made under the most hazardous conditions. It followed Orlando and Cláudio Villas-Boas as they entered previously unexplored areas of the Amazon jungle. They were attempting to locate the Kreen-Akrore tribe[434] and help them make contact with the modern world. The leaders gathered members of other tribes who had once been isolated but who now lived in Parque do Xingu: and set out to make contact. Despite many months of leaving intended gifts for the tribe at one of their banana and maize plantations the expedition failed to make any meaningful contact with the tribe members. The sounds and silences of the forest were often eerie and unsettling; but the photography proved remarkable.[435]

At the same time, there was a long running series on Radio Two called *Music on 2*. Flanders presented four episodes between 1970 and 1972. One episode (20th December) featured the Vienna Boys' Choir[436] and another broadcast on Sunday 25th July 1971 at 8.45 p.m. featured an intriguing bill. First there was a Polish television ballet film which won the 1970 *The Prix Italia*[437]

---

[434] Now known as the Panará people
[435] https://www.cinemaparadiso.co.uk/rentals/the-tribe-that-hides-from-men-56297.html
[436] And again, on 24th December 1972

staged in Florence. *Euridice w*as a paraphrase of the Orpheus and Eurydice myth: it was choreographed by Konrad Drzewiecki to music by J. S. Bach (which was treated electronically by Eugeniusz Rudnik).

This was followed by a recital by soprano Galina Vishnevskaya and Mstislav Rostropovich the celebrated cellist. He was heard in an unusual role when he accompanied his wife in songs by Tchaikovsky and Stravinsky. This was followed by a performance of Bach's Suite No 3, in C major, for unaccompanied cello.[438]

Flanders appeared on BBC One on Christmas Day at 9.00 a.m. He introduced *Christmas Carols* sung by Wandsworth School Choir. Also, Flanders and Swann appeared together on ITV at 9.00 p.m. in the *Val Doonican Christmas Special* (which for several years became a perennial favourite on seasonal television and on which they had appeared two years earlier. They provided a parody of *The Twelve Days of Christmas*.[439]/[440]

---

[437] The Prix Italia was established in Capri in 1948 and was originally dedicated to radio works. From 1957 it also included television productions. Over the years it has been hosted in many of the most famous Italian cities

[438] https://genome.ch.bbc.co.uk/search/0/20?q=music+on+2#top

[439] https://www.imdb.com/title/tt1628671/

[440] https://tvrdb.com/listings/1968-12-25

CHAPTER THIRTEEN
1971 THE FINAL YEARS

Flanders appeared in the film *The Raging Moon*.[441] This was a British romantic drama written and directed by Brian Forbes.[442] Flanders appeared as Clarence Marlow who meets Bruce Pritchard in a convalescent home. He was a vibrant young man whose life is disrupted when he is severely injured during a soccer match and permanently loses the use of both legs. This was broadcast again in 1976 after Flanders' death. The film was not a success at the UK box office;[443] which tells you something.

Flanders later appeared once more as an animals' narrator in two episodes (1971/2) of *The World About Us* – a documentary series with a broad remit of geography, anthropology and natural history subjects. It was created by Sir David Attenborough.

One edition was *The World of Heinz Sielmann*. He was a German wildlife photographer who travelled the world

---

[441] Released in the US as *Long Ago, Tomorrow*
[442] One of UK's most important film makers at the time
[443] https://en.wikipedia.org/wiki/The_Raging_Moon

photographing animals. He pioneered the practice of placing cameras inside birds' nests. His rapid rise to fame came when Peter Scott invited him to show his black and white footage of nesting woodpeckers. To everyone's amazement, immediately after the broadcast, the BBC switchboard was inundated with requests to see the film again. This film is regarded as a classic and earned him a world-wide reputation and he became known as 'Mr Woodpecker.' Sielmann worked with many leading naturalists, all dedicated to the study and understanding of animal behaviour. This was broadcast on Sunday 10th January at 8.15 p.m. on BBC Two.[444]

1971 saw the première[445] of Flanders' well-loved cantata for children *Captain Noah and his Floating Zoo*. He wrote this towards the end of 1970 with composer Joseph Horovitz.[446] The world première in the Queen Elizabeth Hall was on 19th January. It featured the King's Singers; the composer was at the piano. After Flanders' death, this work received the 1976 Ivor Novello Award[447]

---

[444] https://www.imdb.com/title/tt14710318/?ref_=ttfc_fc_cl_i64
[445] https://www.wisemusicclassical.com/news/4175/50th-anniversary-of-Captain-Noah-and-his-Floating-Zoo-by-Joseph-Horovitz/#:~:text=This%20month%20sees%20the%2050,the%20composer%20at%20the%20piano.
[446] Austrian-born British composer and conductor best known for this work which gained great popularity in schools

for the *Best British Work for Children*.[448/449] The work was re-broadcast in June 1979 and once more on Wednesday 26th December 1979 at 1.40 p.m. on Radio 3: over four years after he died.[450]

Although they had known each other for many years, this was the first collaboration between Flanders (who wrote the libretto) and Horovitz. The work was a light-hearted oratorio[451] on the story of Noah; both authors insisted that it was not to be taken as a contribution to what they called 'pop-religion'.

The work has been performed in many different versions and adaptations. Although primarily intended to be sung in schools, in unison or two parts, another version has been prepared by the composer for one soloist; together with a large chorus. The usual accompaniment for jazz trio has been retained and the soloist is the voice of God, the narrator and several other characters as well. The musical style of the cantata is unashamedly eclectic

---

[447] Named after the famous entertainer: awarded for composing and song writing

[448] https://www.wisemusicclassical.com/work/9667/Captain-Noah-and-his-Floating-Zoo--Joseph-Horovitz/

[449] https://ivorsacademy.com/awards/the-ivors/archive/?ay=1976/

[450] https://genome.ch.bbc.co.uk/407dc24c634b4f3686c2c70b5700c3d5

[451] A large-scale musical composition on a sacred subject

and exploits all well-known types of popular music to tell this evergreen story.[452]

Saturday 30th January, Flanders was the narrator in the *Desert War* on Radio 4 at 7.30 p.m. In thirteen parts, this was a series of dramatizations based on the Western Desert Campaign fought in Egypt and Libya during the Second World War.

Flanders and Swann appeared as guests on Radio 2 on Sunday 7th February at 10.01 a.m. on *Eric Robinson: Melodies for you*.

Sunday 16th May there was yet another appearance on *This Week's Good Cause* at 7.25 p.m. on Radio 4: Flanders was obviously a very appealing person. This time for *St Peter's Research Trust*.[453] Established in 1970, this independent trust aimed to raise £50,000 annually for seven years to support research into the prevention, treatment and cure of kidney and bladder disorders.

The same year saw Flanders appear in *Vincent Price is in the Country*: which indeed the American actor, raconteur, art collector and connoisseur of haute cuisine[454]

---

[452] https://www.wisemusicclassical.com/work/9667/Captain-Noah-and-his-Floating-Zoo--Joseph-Horovitz/

[453] Now *The St Peter's Trust*

[454] https://www.imdb.com/name/nm0001637/?ref_=ttfc_fc_cl_t1

was! He hosted a country house party on 1st June which was televised by London Weekend Television.

Monday 7th June the BBC broadcast *Concert Grand* on Radio 2 at 9.15 p.m. in which Flanders and Swann provided piano music: and we assume that Flanders sang.

Friday 9th July at 7.35 p.m. Flanders presented *Llangollen Time* on BBC Wales. You might wonder why time in that part of Wales was so important; the explanation came two days later when he presented *Olé Llangollen* at 2.55 p.m. in which he introduced something of the gaiety, colour and tunefulness of the *International Music Eisteddfod* which was celebrating its silver jubilee that year.

Monday 19th July at 10.10 p.m. saw Flanders and Swann make a guest appearance on *The Spinners*.[455] This was a long running television series broadcast from 1969 to 1983 which featured the Liverpool musicians of that name. The Spinners sang 'songs you have known all your life and songs you may have never heard before;' so they were all embracing. Flanders and Swann sang their song written for today's 'permissive society' and raised the roof with *The Hippopotamus Song*.[456]

---

[455] They began as a skiffle group and later began singing sea shanties
[456] https://genome.ch.bbc.co.uk/schedules/service_bbc_one_london/1971

Friday 30th July Flanders appeared on *Sounds Familiar* on Radio 4 at 4.00 p.m. This was a panel game that turned the pages of showbiz history. Along with Flanders this edition featured Dinah Sheridan,[457] Ian Wallace and Dick Vosburgh (the latter was an American-born comedy writer and lyricist who worked chiefly in Britain).

On Friday 3rd September at 8.00 p.m., BBC Two - in *Daphne du Maurier's Vanishing Cornwall* - set out to find an answer to an interesting question: why is Cornwall different? The programme was directed by du Maurier's son; Flanders was the narrator for the programme which addressed that question; we do not know for sure whether he answered it. The programme considered what it was about the county's history and people, their customs, superstitions and legends that had given the peninsula a feeling that it was almost a foreign country.

-07-19
[457] She played Wendy McKim in Genevieve

Flanders and Swann provide piano music

Wednesday 15th September at 9.00 p.m. on Radio 4 Flanders appeared in *Now Read On* in which he introduced news of books and writers. Graham Green talked about his autobiography *A Sort of Life* and Flanders' old mucker Sir Peter Ustinov read an extract from his novel *Krumnagel*. He appeared in the programme again on Wednesday 22nd September and 6th October 1971; presenting what was, at the time, a regular programme of book reviews. In one edition the Irish actress and author Eileen O'Casey talked about her biography of her husband the Irish dramatist Seán O'Casey.

On Friday 8th October Flanders presented *Kyung-Wha Chung* on BBC One at 11.00 p.m. This programme featured a young[458] Korean violinist who was making her British television concert debut playing the *Mendelssohn Violin Concerto* with the London Symphony Orchestra, leader John Georgiadis[459] and conducted by André Previn KBE. The programme included *Brahms's Variations on a theme of Haydn*. Flanders introduced several later programmes featuring this talented violinist.

Saturday 9th October at 9.35 p.m. on BBC Two Flanders was the commentator for the *Moscow State Circus*[460] in the BBC series *Wide World of Entertainment*.

---

[458] Now 75! She is recognized as one of the finest violinists of her generation

[459] British violinist and conductor

It was the first visit to the UK[461] for eleven years of this famous circus and forty stars of Russian circus thrilled their British audiences. Among other things their famous clown Oleg Popov talked about the circus. He introduced many of the acts. Alas we may not see them again; thanks to Mr Putin.

1972

Flanders was a perfectly competent actor; although he was in no state to play James Bond (even allowing for the rather cruel newspaper which did a cartoon of Roger Moore in a wheelchair for his last Bond outing). However, he could easily do the sort of part where the character was naturally sitting down. This primarily meant radio, but there is the slightly odd (and all too brief) moment in *Doctor in Distress*[462] where the audience is left to gaze at a character and mutter to themselves: "Is that Michael Flanders?" having not seen him in colour before (the record sleeves in which his LPs were published were inclined towards monochrome and it would of course be

---

[460] The name has long been used generically by troupes of Russian circus performers in the West
[461] At Wembley
[462] He played Bradby

heresy to produce a new colour one).[463] In the film he was complete with his familiar little grin and mannerisms.

Sunday 2nd January at 8.15 p.m. BBC One broadcast *The Great Stars: Doctor in Distress*. This was the first of three films honouring Dirk Bogarde: one of Britain's most distinguished actors. Flanders had appeared in the fifth of the seven *Doctor* films (made in 1963).

As noted earlier, Flanders appeared as narrator in two episodes of *The World About Us*. The second was *Flamenco Triangle* on 23rd January on BBC Two at 8.25 p.m.[464] In this episode he considered that deep in the south-west corner of Spain lay one of the most fascinating regions in Europe, the *Flamenco Triangle*. It is a land shared by both colourful people and wild life; their lives strongly intertwined. The programme questioned what would happen to this land of bulls and horses, flamingos and eagles; flamenco and fiesta? Flanders seemed to be entwined with flamingos: but did not write a song about them.

The 26th January was a big day as Flanders was featured as the celebrity guest on *This Is Your Life*. He was surprised by Eamonn Andrews at Thames

---

[463] https://thegawain.wordpress.com/2013/03/11/flanders-and-swann/
[464] Repeated in July 1973

Television's Euston Road Studios.[465] He was there because he had been led to believe that he was going to be interviewed about a new show.[466] The episode was broadcast live.

Those appearing were:

- Lister Welch (actor and stage director)
- Dick Vosburgh (American comedy writer)
- Courtney Kenny (Irish musician)
- Claudia - wife
- Donald Swann
- Val Doonican
- Anthony Wedgwood Benn
- Peter - father
- Pat - sister
- Rosemary - sister
- John Anderson (American character actor)
- George Marchant
- Sister Rebecca McRae
- Sister Peggy Nugent
- Ian Wallace (Actor)

---

[465] Opened 1969: *Thames Television House*
[466] https://www.bigredbook.info/michael_flanders.html

- The Spinners (Liverpool folk music band)
- Laura - daughter
- Stephanie - daughter[467]

One heroic appearance was on Sunday 12th March at 11.10 a.m. on Radio 4 when Flanders again fronted *This Week's Good Cause*. This time the appeal was on behalf of *Action for the Crippled Child*.[468] The charity was originally founded by Duncan Guthrie, who made it his mission to raise funds to defeat polio, a condition that (as we understand by now) affected the lives of many thousands of children including Guthrie's own daughter Janet.

Flanders was often seen on the concert platform. One appearance was alongside members of the Academy of St Martin-in-the-Fields with Fenella Fielding in 1972 in a production of Edith Sitwell's *Façade*; an entertainment with poems; with Sir William Walton's music.[469]

Walton was a notable English composer: especially known for his orchestral music. In the period between the time of Vaughan Williams and Benjamin Britten,

---

[467] https://www.bigredbook.info/michael_flanders.html
[468] Now *Action Medical Research*
[469] Available on an EMI LP

Walton's early work made him one of England's most important composers.

Flanders said that he had long been fascinated by *Façade*. He remarked "It is an extraordinarily difficult work. There are times when you are just forced to babble, others when you are completely swamped by the orchestra. It really pushes you to the limits." This was broadcast on *Showcase* on Monday 20th March at 4.40 p.m. on Radio 3.

In quick succession on Wednesday 29th March Flanders appeared on BBC Two at 9.20 p.m. in *Walton at 70*. This was an affectionate tribute to Sir William Walton[470] from some of his friends to mark his seventieth birthday. It was introduced by John Amis with excerpts (again) from *Façade*: with Flanders, Fenella Fielding and the Nash Ensemble;[471] and *Five Bagatelles for Guitar*[472] played by Julian Bream.

Sunday 28th May at 7.30 p.m. on Radio 4 residents of the RNIB Home for the Blind at Westgate-on-Sea (together with students from the Dorton House School for the Blind at Sevenoaks) put questions about religion to a panel including Flanders in *Questions of Belief*. One other

---

[470] Died 1983
[471] English chamber ensemble founded 1964
[472] His only work for guitar

contributor was David Scott Blackhall: he was a radio personality and author who had gone completely blind by the time he was forty-five but mastered braille in three weeks.

Flanders and Swann appeared in *There Was an Englishman, an Irishman, and a Scotsman* on Monday 5th June at 8.00 p.m. on Radio 4. Famous for their wonderfully clever national song *A Song of Patriotic Prejudice*, they were naturals to appear in a broadcast which set out to present a comic tour of the British Isles guided by Frank Muir: which that week stopped in Wales and the West Country. This was repeated on 5th September at 6.15 p.m.

Flanders appeared in one episode of *Music on 2 – the Best of Counterpoint* on Sunday 16th July on BBC Two at 9.00 p.m. Flanders was a performer on a programme that was devised (yet again) by John Amis.

Sunday 27th August Flanders and Swann appeared in a bank holiday anthology of readings and records on Radio 4 at 6.15 p.m. in *How Hot the Sun Was*. It was introduced by Jean Metcalfe.

1973

With animals in mind, on 11th January at 7.35 p.m. on BBC Two Flanders was the narrator in *The Web of Life – The Living Savanna*. This was the second of six films that showed the beautiful intertwining of the living things on our varied earth. It focussed on the big game of East Africa: lion, leopard, cheetah, hyena, elephant, giraffe, zebra and antelope. It questioned how dependent each breed was on the others.[473]

On the 15th April, Flanders was back on *This Week's Good Cause* this time appealing on behalf of the *Disabled Living Foundation*. This had been founded in 1969 and to this day works to improve the daily lives of anyone disabled from any cause; whether mental or physical.

The *Animal Game* was a Sunday afternoon panel quiz on BBC One at 2.15 p.m. broadcast from Bristol. This was a new kind of quiz in which professional and amateur experts faced a series of wildlife questions. Among others Flanders appeared with Johnny Morris in four episodes in 1973 because of his association with animals; vis a vis *The Bestiary*.[474] The last programme in the first series was broadcast on the 29th April.

---

[473] https://genome.ch.bbc.co.uk/search/0/20?q=web+of+life#top
[474] https://www.imdb.com/title/tt9773794/

As we have noted, Flanders had become a frequent guest on quiz shows. In the famous Radio 4 quiz show *Twenty Questions*, Gilbert Harding was Chairman: he was a onetime scholar, policeman, teacher, journalist, BBC editor and irascible eccentric. Harding harangued a panel of celebrities who had to identify a mystery object within twenty questions. A typical riddle might have been malt whisky or a female weightlifter.

Harding once got very drunk on the show. He had brought producer Ian Messiter a triple gin and tonic to 'loosen him up' before recording. Messiter refused it so Harding drank the lot - probably on top of what he had already consumed. During the twenty-seven minutes the programme was on the air he managed to insult Richard Dimbleby (as "The BBC's sacred cow"), Joy Adamson ("Joy by name, but not by nature") and failed to recognise that the panel had correctly identified "a peony" after question seven and went on to announce the answer - to much commotion - after twenty questions. Harding barked back: "Serves them right - they should not take this silly game so seriously. Let's get on with the next object." He closed the programme three minutes early with the diatribe: "I'm fed up with this idiotic game; as for the score, if you've been listening you won't need it; if you haven't, you won't want it. I'm going home." It was of course utterly splendid radio.

Accordingly, Flanders took over as Chairman in 1973.[475] He was probably the first ever game show host in a wheelchair. As an example, on Wednesday 13th June at 6.15 p.m. Flanders was in the Chair and Anona Winn and Norman Hackforth were among those making up the panel.

Wednesday 28th November at 7.30 p.m. on Radio 4 there was a splendid programme entitled *Celebration* in which Flanders and Swann celebrated a quarter of a century of writing songs for revues.

1974

The year saw the publication of yet another book - *The Sayings and Doings of Nasrudin the Wise*. This was a children's book published by Studio Vista[476] and comprised thirteen very short tales each with colour illustrations by the Turkish designer Yurdaer Altintas.

17th February, Flanders introduced *Martha Argerich* on BBC Two at 9.00 p.m. The programme featured the

---

[475] http://www.ukgameshows.com/ukgs/Twenty_Questions
[476] Owned by Collier Macmillan

young South American pianist and she played *Chopin's 24 Preludes*.[477]

Flanders and Swann were reunited for a radio programme *The Best of Flanders and Swann* broadcast on 3rd March at 6.15 p.m. on Radio 4. They reminisced about their past triumphs together. Fourteen months later the programme was re-broadcast on 21st May 1975 at 7.30 p.m. in tribute to Flanders; who had then died recently.

---

[477] His 24 Preludes, Op. 28 are a set of short pieces for the piano; one in each of the twenty-four keys

Nasrudin the Wise

Sunday 10th March Flanders had a very interesting task: he was narrator on a Radio 2 programme (in four instalments) at 2.30 p.m. telling the the *Henry Hall Story*. Almost forgotten today, Hall was a famous (fame is very transient!) English bandleader. The programme discussed his career with many recording artistes from the world of music, including Benno Moiseiwitsch[478] and Harriet Cohen.

What's It All About? was a quiz show based on religion (unlikely as that idea might sound). Two participants each week were from a religious seminary and the third was a celebrity belonging to a similar religion (except for the last series, when Peter Moloney and popular Irish singer Dana were the permanent captains). Moloney was a former Trappist monk, an African missionary and a polymath; he enjoyed a brief television career starring in shows including *What's It All About*? Flanders was a stand in as celebrity host for two episodes because Joan Bakewell was taken ill part way through the 1974 series. So, the semi-finals and final were presented by Flanders:[479] one on Sunday 31st March at 6.50 p.m. the other on the 7th

---

[478] Russian born British pianist

[479] http://www.ukgameshows.com/ukgs/What%27s_it_All_About%3F_(2)

April. Incidentally: two things. Firstly, one member of the celebrity panel in the first series was none other than Jimmy Saville. Secondly, Swann says that at school Flanders' interest in religion was 'very peripheral:'[480] so what?

Wednesday 3rd April at 11.05 a.m. - and throughout the rest of the year - the BBC broadcaster, writer and raconteur Frank Muir investigated a whole multitude of diverse subjects such as Frank *Muir goes into ------ hobbies:* and later of all things *Lust* and *Holidays* among other diverse subjects. The programme investigated these subjects with many voices including frequently those of Flanders and Swann.[481]

Flanders, this most appealing broadcaster, was back on the radio on *This Week's Good Cause* on Sunday 27th October when he sought funds for *The Outset Foundation,* which recruits and organises volunteers for community service projects: with a particular focus on helping the elderly, the disabled and the homeless.[482]

November saw the publication of *The Sloth and The Gnu* published by Frederick Warne and Company[483]

---

[480] Swann, Donald. Op. cit. p. 61
[481] https://genome.ch.bbc.co.uk/66feecbfe45b4981afb5023ca7b9319a
[482] https://genome.ch.bbc.co.uk/search/100/20?q=Michael+Flanders#top

(known for their children's books) in the *stuff and nonsense* genre.

Wednesday 18th December on Radio 3 at 6.30 p.m. Flanders and Swann appeared in *Study on 3* on which they promoted *And Then We Wrote*.

As noted earlier, after *At the Drop of Another Hat* was over there were thoughts about a third show to be called *Hat Trick*. Instead, the pair were not reunited until they came together with some old friends for *And Then We Wrote*. On 16th May they went into the BBC Paris Theatre[484]/[485] and recorded this retrospective. This was published by EMI in 1975 - one of a collection of albums gathering up pieces not in the main *Hat* recordings. The others were *Bestiary* and *Tried by the Centre Court*; the former sticks to animal songs while the latter is a rather mixed bag of the best tape-based recordings and cutting-room-floor bits from the commercial recordings. It represents the first time that a Sydney Carter song performed by Flanders and Swann, *The Youth of the Heart*, made it to a commercial release.

---

[483] Later acquired by Penguin Books
[484] Originally a cinema located at 12 Lower Regent Street. Converted into a studio for radio broadcasts requiring an audience: closed in 1995
[485] Berger, Leon: *Hat-Tricks: guide to the songs*

And Then We Wrote was broadcast on Radio 4 on Tuesday 24th December 1974 at 7.30 p.m. Flanders and Swann invited listeners to an on-air party to hear how some of their hitherto unrecorded hit songs came to be written. With the help of some of their dear chums (Pat Lancaster, Charlotte Mitchell, Anne Rogers and Julian Orchard) they ran through some pre-*Drop of a Hat* revue numbers from *Oranges and Lemons, Penny Plain, Airs on a Shoestring* and *Fresh Airs*. It may have been their last joint broadcast.

CHAPTER FOURTEEN
1975

So began the last year of Flanders' life. Sunday 12th January at 10.05 p.m. on BBC One Flanders introduced a *Royal Concert*: one of his last major appearances. He introduced part of the annual concert celebrating the *Festival of St Cecilia*:[486] an event which has been the flagship in *Help Musicians'* calendar since 1946. Musicians come together to celebrate what music brings to everyone. It had been held the previous November at the Royal Albert Hall in the presence of HM Queen Elizabeth the Queen Mother.

The Russian-American concert pianist, Shura Cherkassky played *Piano Concerto No 1 by Liszt,* Sheila Armstrong sang Mozart's concert aria, *Ch'io mi scordi di te* and Raymond Leppard conducted the Royal Philharmonic Orchestra in Holst's Ballet Suite: *The Perfect Fool*. To top it off, trumpeters of the Royal

---

[486] Patron of musicians, composers, instrument makers and poets

Military School of Music opened the concert with a Fanfare and the National Anthem.

Children of the 1970s will remember Flanders' voice as narrator on the soundtrack of the *Barbapapa* animated cartoon series. This followed the daily lives of the extraordinary blob-shaped Barbapapa family, who can morph into other forms but retain their original colours. The family consists of parents Barbapapa and Barbamama and their seven children. *Barbapapa* has had a total of five English dubs. The first aired on BBC One in the UK from 17th January 1975 at 4.45 p.m.[487] it was given many airings later.

On Sunday 2nd February at 9.05 p.m. on BBC Two, Flanders introduced *Music of Fritz Kreisler*. He was an Austrian born American violinist (one of the most noted of his day) and composer. The programme paid tribute to him on the centenary of his birth. The recital included arrangements and original compositions including *Caprice Viennois*, *Schon Rosmarin* and *Tambourin Chinois*.[488] It was his finale: and we never saw his like again.

---

[487] https://dubbing.fandom.com/wiki/Barbapapa

[488] https://genome.ch.bbc.co.uk/a28242bcb43d4506854003a315bd68bd

CHAPTER FIFTEEN
THE END

Flanders died suddenly on 14th April 1975 of a ruptured intracranial berry aneurysm.[489] He was in an isolated guest house in Wales while on holiday at Betws-y-Coed (the name means *prayer house in the wood*). It is a small place in the Conwyn Valley in Caernarfonshire on the boundary with Denbighshire.

He had told the owners that it was the first place that he had stayed where nobody knew him. Flanders always had to exert himself tremendously getting in and out of bed. His doctors expected his early death.[490]

His ashes were scattered in the grounds of Chiswick House, London,[491] where he had loved to sit in the afternoon. Flanders' memorial was held at St Martin-in-the- Fields on 14th June 1975.

---

[489] When a berry aneurysm ruptures, blood from the artery moves into the brain

[490] Swann, Donald. Op. cit. p. 195-7

[491] The architect and designer William Kent and his friend and patron the third Earl of Burlington, created the House and Gardens between 1725 and about 1738

His wife Claudia built on the experience she had gained accompanying her husband on the Flanders and Swann tours and became an expert herself in making transport accessible to disabled people. She remained close to Swann after her husband's death and held countless musical parties at which Swann would accompany distinguished performers presenting Flanders and Swann songs.[492]

After his death, Claudia was asked to open the *Michael Flanders Resource Centre* for day care in Acton. The aim being to enable older people with substantial and critical needs to remain living in their own homes: their being supported with a variety of day opportunities tailored to their individual needs *and* in a dignified manner.[493]

Later, Stephanie Flanders made a Radio 4 programme about her father in 2007 and wrote about it for BBC News in an article *Rediscovering My Father*.[494] How sad for her that she was so young when he died that she had to *rediscover* him.

---

[492] https://www.independent.co.uk/arts-entertainment/obituary-claudia-flanders-1173922.html

[493] Fhttps://healthwatchealing.org.uk/services/michael-flanders-centre-london-w3-8pp/

[494] http://news.bbc.co.uk/1/hi/magazine/6253824.stm

Flanders' last book *Golf Talk: The Greatest Things Ever Said About the Game of Golf* was published by Click Books in the August after his death. This was a collection of quotations that celebrated the endless fascinations of the game. It was suggested that never before had so many thoughts about golf been compiled into one volume. It contained a treasure trove of quotations, humorous anecdotes and philosophical insights collected and selected by the great man himself.[495] Copies fetch a good price today.

In 1989 the BBC broadcast *Buses, Gasmen and Hippos* on Radio 2 at 9.00 p.m. in fond remembrance of Flanders. Ian Wallace looked back affectionately at their many successes with John Amis, Tony Benn, John Bridges, Sydney Carter, Claudia Flanders, Rose Hill, Joseph Horovitz, George Martin, Donald Swann and Sandy Wilson.

At the end of 1994, the year of Swann's death,[496] on the 27th December the BBC broadcast *Flanders and Swann* on BBC Two at 6.50 p.m. It was a warm tribute to a much-loved duo. It was presented by their old friend, patron and supporter John Amis. He told stories and

---

[495] https://www.goodreads.com/book/show/12123102-golf-talk
[496] Broadcast on PBS in 1998

introduced clips of them performing. It was an affectionate look back at the song writing and performing partnership. The programme featured a compilation of then recently discovered archive recordings of performances given on Broadway.[497]

On 14th January 1996 on Radio 2 at 10.00 p.m. Flanders and Swann were featured (along with Gracie Fields, George Formby, Joyce Grenfell, Tony Hancock, Max Miller, Peter Sellers, Peter Ustinov and Kenneth Williams among many others) in *One Hundred Years of British Comedy*.

As one speaker commented in a documentary some years ago, something has been missing since 1967: the lyrical skill: humour: musical proficiency: intimacy: sublime sophistication[498] and a joy of being English.

Flanders' and Swann's unique brand of comedy still delights many all over the world. Their songs utilized witty puns and wonderful word play: they were perhaps some of the least political and controversial of the era because they talked about everyday problems.[499] With over

---

[497] https://genome.ch.bbc.co.uk/schedules/service_bbc_two_england/1994-12-27

[498] An understanding of the world and its ways; and of the way people behave

[499] https://everything2.com/title/Flanders+and+Swann

two thousand live performances, which featured the most successful musical comedy songs of a generation Flanders and Swann occupy a very special place.[500]

---

[500] https://flandersandswann.info/originals/

CHAPTER SIXTEEN
TRIBUTES

English Heritage unveiled a Blue Plaque in Kensington on 5th September 2018 at No. 1 Scarsdale Villas[501/502] where Flanders and Swann wrote their early material. There was no car with a number plate GNU parked outside at the time.

---

[501] https://www.londonremembers.com/memorials/flanders-and-swann
[502] 'Turn left by Ponting's dustbins'

Flanders' life and work was further celebrated at the *Chiswick Book Festival* in 2022.[503] On 14th September, the *Ealing Civic Trust* unveiled a green plaque at 63 Esmond Road, Chiswick: where Flanders lived from 1971 to 1975. It was his home together with his wife and two daughters (both of whom are now prominent journalists). There was an event that evening - *Celebrating Michael Flanders (& Swann)* - in the Old Library: not far from the *Michael Flanders Centre* in Church Street, which Claudia opened in his honour after his death and which was sponsored by the British Comedy Guide.[504] Stephanie and Laura Flanders discussed their father's impact on comedy and the world of disability with *Comedy Chronicles* writer Graham McCann and the Festival director, Torin Douglas.[505]

---

[503] https://www.chiswickbookfestival.net/celebrating-the-legacy-of-michael-flanders/

[504] https://www.ticketsource.co.uk/whats-on/the-old-library-high-st-acton-w3-6na/actone-cinema-cafe/celebrating-michael-flanders-swann/e-epvjrj

[505] https://commons.wikimedia.org/wiki/File:Chiswick_Book_Festival_2022_Celebrating_Michael_Flanders_(%26_Swann)_(52358424044).jpg

The Chiswick Book Festival also added Flanders to its *WRITER'S TRAIL*[506] - which celebrates notable novelists, playwrights, poets and lyricists who have lived in the area.

> EALING CIVIC SOCIETY
> **MICHAEL FLANDERS** OBE
> 1922 – 1975
> ACTOR, SONGWRITER, PERFORMER, BROADCASTER
> Lived here
> 1971 – 1975

---

[506] https://www.chiswickbookfestival.net/chiswick-timeline-writers-trail/

CHAPTER SEVENTEEN
DISABILITY

Flanders proved that you could overcome adversity. In 1966 Walter Kerr in *The New York Times* put it this way: "Flanders . . . skates about the stage as though his wheelchair were a swan boat in the process of making figure eights along the road to Valhalla."[507] Swann remarked that Flanders reached a point where he had total command from a seated position: he had worked out to a fine art how to function on stage.[508]

Berger said "I think the fact you've got Flanders in a wheelchair sitting up on stage is pretty pioneering; I can't think[509] of a single example, certainly not in the UK, of a public figure who's been disabled."[510]

Flanders faced many difficulties as a performer in a wheelchair and he was devastated that despite the fact he

---

[507] https://www.nytimes.com/1975/04/16/archives/michael-flanders-is-dead-at-53-humoriststar-of-drop-of-a-hat.html
[508] Swann, Donald. Op. cit. p. 133
[509] But he had not thought of Franklin D. Roosevelt
[510] Berger is currently writing the authorized biography of Flanders and Swann. https://leon-berger.com/writer/

could perform, other wheelchair users were not permitted in the theatre. Swann reported that "enormous attention" was paid to ensuring Flanders' access to the theatre, but that the same courtesy was not provided to the audience. In Swann's words, "The ironic thing was that in those days disabled people could not come to the theatre as there were lots of rules and regulations and no provision whatsoever for them. What a ludicrous thing: he could play but others could not watch him!"[511] Flanders said "Nobody is interested in how you got here; but, for a disabled person, that you got here at all is an achievement."[512]

Accordingly, and unusually for the time, neither Flanders or Swann stood during their shows; Swann being seated at the piano and Flanders confined to a wheelchair.[513] While the difficulty of being in a wheelchair in the theatre may not have been obvious on stage, behind the scenes was another matter. Swann noted that the New Lindsey had three stage hands whose "~~~ only job was to lift Flanders down the stairs backstage and up again. Once they dropped him and he nearly had concussion. It was all

---

[511] https://www.filmedlivemusicals.com/at-the-drop-hat.html
[512] https://www.independent.co.uk/arts-entertainment/obituary-claudia-flanders-1173922.html
[513] https://tropedia.fandom.com/wiki/Flanders_and_Swann

very primitive: he could not get into a dressing room so he had a rudimentary curtained cubicle just off-stage with a simple mirror. Everything was measured down to the last detail to map where he could go."

Stephanie Flanders' relates that her early childhood was dominated by an awareness of steps and the height of light switches. "I don't think I ever grew out of looking at things through the eyes of someone in a wheelchair. We went to beautiful old towns in France where anyone else would have admired the wonderful cobbled streets. But our hearts would sink because cobbles are the worst thing if you are in a wheelchair. We were all, in a way, looking after him. He was at the centre of things."[514]

So, Flanders became a passionate advocate for the rights of people with disabilities, a cause with which his wife Claudia also became heavily involved. She died in 1998 and had spent more than twenty years working for disabled people after the death of her husband. Her uncle Patrick Cockburn (Middle East correspondent for *The Independent*) had also survived a childhood bout of polio.[515]

---

[514] https://www.telegraph.co.uk/culture/tvandradio/3587226/Ill-give-as-good-as-I-get.html
[515] https://www.independent.co.uk/arts-entertainment/tv/reviews/the-battle-to-beat-polio-bbc2-tv-review-home-truths-from-stephanie-flanders-in-a-revealing-look-at-the-fight-against-polio-9399197.html

Mrs Flanders was awarded an Order of the British Empire in 1981 for her work:[516] and her husband would have been inordinately proud of her. Swann commented that Claudia was outstanding in that field. Following Flanders' death, she founded the charity *Tripscope* to champion better transport and access for the disabled:[517] (it was wound up in 2006).[518]

Stephanie Flanders wrote that as a child she recalled touring the country on her mother's campaigns. "There are countless local newspaper pictures of me in toilets, measuring the width of seats and doors while my mother talked about accessibility with local celebrities. Like her much-lamented husband, she was a very outgoing, gregarious woman and she nagged transport officials all the time. I am not sure they quite knew what to do with this American firebrand."[519] Well, they wouldn't would they.

---

[516] https://www.filmedlivemusicals.com/blog/up-close-with-flanders-swann
[517] https://www.independent.co.uk/arts-entertainment/obituary-claudia-flanders-1173922.html
[518] https://register-of-charities.charitycommission.gov.uk/charity-details/?regid=294559&subid=0
[519] https://www.telegraph.co.uk/culture/tvandradio/3587226/Ill-give-as-good-as-I-get.html

CHAPTER EIGHTEEN
ENCORE

McCann bemoans the fact that Flanders and Swann do not get heard much these days. But he suggests that[520] over the last sixty years they have made a profound and lasting impact not only on British comedy and music, but also on almost every other major point and place in the panorama of British entertainment. From many genre (and he instances from *Beyond the Fringe* to *That Was the Week That Was*) there are significant cultural strands stretching back specifically to the teamwork of these two great men.

The pair, like Armstrong and Miller,[521] were rather posh, but they were left-wing rather than right and their humour was appreciated by all kinds of audiences right across the social class scale. They were also the masters of a kind of witty and wry style of self- depreciation. They made Britain smile - *and think* - when it really needed to

---

[520] https://www.comedy.co.uk/features/comedy_chronicles/remarkable-legacy-of-flanders-and-swann/

[521] English comedy act

do both at the same time. Their deprecation set the tone for post-war and post-colonial English irony. *At the Drop of a Hat*, therefore, offered the kind of intelligence and irreverence that struck a chord and resonated right through the whole country: perhaps even through the empire!

They were responding to the Fifties, but anticipating the Sixties and were inspiring all sorts of people as they did so. Sibley recalls that he was totally mesmerised by the witty lyrics of Flanders and the instantly memorable music of Swann; performed in their contrasting - but complementary - baritone and tenor voices with unflagging zest and verve.[522] They transcended any class, age, gender, ethnic or regional divisions of the time and, without compromising their craft, genuinely entertained the whole nation, rather than any particular niche. 'There is really no need to introduce Flanders and Swann to the North-East public,' declared the *Newcastle Chronicle* in 1962. 'They are household words, like fish and chips, tripe and onions, and Tyne and tide'.[523] Flanders, notwithstanding his difficult circumstances, maintained an unchallenged warmth and urbanity.[524]

---

[522] http://briansibleysblog.blogspot.com/2008/02/who-says-nostalgia-isnt-what-it-was.html
[523] Op. cit
[524] 1975, *The Times*, London, obituary

Their music lives on: even endures! It is good that thirty-four years after Flanders' death, Paul Gambaccini featured *At the Drop of a Hat* on *One Night Only* on Radio 4 in 2009.[525] He described the show as 'a quintessentially English evening' and that it was 'the show at which to be seen: it had the blessing of the young set: everyone came: they did it better than anyone else:' and they were described as just *two men and a piano*. That famous wheelchair might have been included!

Their songs have been used on film soundtracks like *The Last Post* TV mini-series and the *Wicker Tree*.[526] Archive footage was seen of him in 2015 in his famous programme about Kenneth More.[527]

Australians thought that to the Americans Flanders and Swann were explosively funny. lively witty and daffy:[528]/[529] to the British they were neat and smart.[530]

---

[525] https://www.bbc.co.uk/programmes/b00d1025
[526] https://www.bbc.co.uk/programmes/b09dcvzl
[527] https://www.imdb.com/title/tt5953662/?ref_=nm_flmg_arf_1
[528] https://trove.nla.gov.au/newspaper/article/265922179?searchTerm=Michael%20Flanders
[529] Silly, mildly eccentric
[530] Op. cit

CHAPTER NINETEEN
THE SONGS

Flanders was very much against his songs being printed: but they *were* published after his death and it then transpired that Swann had not committed the music to paper: so only the words appeared in print.[531]

A search of the out-takes and private tapes made of the shows following Swann's death turned up various interesting results, including some pieces from their days at Oxford; the resulting cluster of songs and sketches were released in 2007 as *Hat Trick: Flanders and Swann Collector's Edition*. This chapter is grounded in the wonderful guide to their songs written for **Hat Trick**: which is a ***must buy*** for any enthusiast. It was written masterfully by **Leon Berger**.

By Air has Flanders giving a humorous preamble about the pleasures and tribulations of flying, with each well-crafted gag getting a laugh of recognition from an audience that was made up of folk from that first

---

[531] Amis, John: sleeve notes for *The Complete Flanders and Swann* CD set

generation in Britain for whom air travel was starting to be a fairly regular pursuit. Flanders pokes fun at the petty indignities of getting to the airport and negotiating your way around it once there: the absurd language of instruction ("Beware of low-flying aircraft"), the petty rules and regulations, the impenetrability of announcements, the special challenges faced by one such as Flanders who was in a wheelchair (he recalls being raised up to the plane by a fork lift – "why they need a great machine like that just to lift forks I don't know"). In the end he says that he agrees with the old lady who said that "If God had intended us to fly, he would never have given us the railways;" and so they sing a song about railway stations instead.[532]

In the *Bonus Disc* in this set, Flanders amused himself spoofing nightly news bulletins with a skit that has outlived most, if not all, of the original bulletins. Swann, meanwhile, did a straight version of his setting of *Je Suis Le Tenebreux* (which it is widely agreed is rather spoilt by translation). Also, to be found in this bundle of stuff is a song about the girls of St Trinian's School[533] – of all the people to encounter in what initially seems from this

---

[532] https://lukemckernan.com/2018/03/08/by-air/
[533] Fictional: anarchic school for uncontrollable girls

distance like a high-brow form of show. With some polishing, gathering together and arranging, these additional songs appeared in *And Then We Wrote* and the original release of *At the Drop of a Hat*. In the process we get to see how Flanders and Swann developed over the years.

The collection results in some duplication (*Pillar to Post appears* twice and *Grandma* three times in various formats – this is Flanders' *Grandma*, not the one that a school choir sang about in 1980; but along the way a couple of the songs only referenced in *And Then We Wrote* actually get to appear in full. *Survival of the Phew* was written off as "rather long and boring" but is still nice to hear at length, while *Rain on the Plage* is a magnificently soft tune catching the mood of sitting in a cafe watching the rain drum down outside.[534]

Berger draws attention to perhaps the most poignant lyric that Flanders ever wrote (of the armadillo):[535] *Never tell a man the truth about the one that he adores.* Mind you, this line is almost matched by all the lines in *Slow Train*. They represent an almost continuous lament for all the railway stations lost as a result of the Beeching Axe. It

---

[534] https://thegawain.wordpress.com/2013/03/11/flanders-and-swann/
[535] Berger, Leon: *Hat-Tricks: guide to the songs*

is a wistful retrospective: one not intended to be comic on any level. It regrets the passing of all these wonderful station names of the 19th century railways.[536]

The plaintive echoes in a love song to a pillar box *Pillar to Post* ("pity the poor little pillar box)" resonate: as do the lyrics of *The Man from Aix-les-Bains* ("Call me Uncle Joe"): we have all met one of those bores on holiday.

They were very topical. Listening to their '50s recordings provides listeners with a real flavour of the time. (We're terribly *House and Garden* (the famous magazine for which Flanders' sister worked mentioned along with the new-fangled eye level grill) in *Design for Living*). The introduction to *Greensleeves* refers to *angry young men* of which there was an abundance in the mid '50s. Their work was laced with social comment.[537] An over-riding example was *There's a Hole in my Budget* which they updated over a dozen years to fit the approaches of different Chancellors and Premiers as they came and went.

---

[536] https://thegawain.wordpress.com/2013/03/11/flanders-and-swann/
[537] Amis, John: sleeve notes for *The Complete Flanders and Swann* CD set

Flanders' lyrics were also sometimes quite racy by the mores of the staid fifties. He sang that in Tonga "Oly-ma-kitty-luca-chi-chi-chi" meant "No" and if he ever had the money it would be to Tonga he would go and by the time a girl said "Oly-ma-kitty-luca-chi-chi-chi" it would probably be too late. Amis reminds us that the original ending to *Satellite Moon* was "the girl in my arms is a boy:"[538] a line which would have infuriated puritans. There is one recording in existence with this original lyric.

Another of his favourite songs was *Madeira* (an exercise in Zeugma) in which the Wardrobe Mistress brought on his hat: and he told the audience not to take her title too literally.

Perhaps Amis summed it up the best when he described Flanders' and Swann's contribution. He described them as good chaps who wrote good lyrics and tunes: delivered with wit and imagination. In addition, he said, they treated the audience as literates.[539]

---

[538] Op. cit

[539] Amis, John: sleeve notes for *The Complete Flanders and Swann* CD set

ALSO BY RICHARD R. DOLPHIN:

COLLECTING BEER CANS
1977, Trewin Copplestone Publishing Ltd

THE INTERNATIONAL BOOK OF BEER CAN COLLECTING
1977, Hamlyn Publishing Group Ltd
4 impressions in UK and USA

FIRE POWER
1992, private publication by St Andrews Church, West Hatch

THE FUNDAMENTALS OF CORPORATE COMMUNICATIONS
1998, Butterworth-Heinemann

THROUGH ALL THE CHANGING SCENES OF LIFE
2018, Amazon

A PROUD PHOENIX FLEW OVER WEST HATCH
2019, Amazon

SWEET INSPIRATIONS
2019, Amazon

FROM THE SCYTHIA TO SUNDERLAND
THE GOLDEN LIFE OF TOMMY STEELE
2020, Amazon

FOXHUNTERS
2021, Amazon

VERY LOVELY PEOPLE
2022, Amazon

AND THEN THERE WERE FOUR
2022, Amazon

Printed in Great Britain
by Amazon